SOUTH STAFFORDSHIRE
'REVIEWED'

*A nostalgic photographic survey produced on the occasion
of South Staffordshire Council's 30th Anniversary*

SOUTH STAFFORDSHIRE
'REVIEWED'

A nostalgic photographic survey produced on the occasion
of South Staffordshire Council's 30th Anniversary

by

Paul Collins & Craig Walker

A South Staffordshire Council Publication

South Staffordshire Council, Council Offices, Wolverhampton Road, Codsall. WV8 1PX

British Library Cataloguing in Publication Data
Data available

Library of Congress Cataloguing in Publication Data
Data available

ISBN 0-9547984-0-6

Typeset by Craig Walker
Printed in England by Simlex Group Limited

CONTENTS

INTRODUCTION

South Staffordshire Council came into being on 1 April 1974. It was one of many new local authorities that day, all of which were created by the reforms embodied in the Local Government Act, 1972. The new council was a marriage between two predecessor authorities: Cannock Rural District Council and Seisdon Rural District Council. A previous Local Government Act, of 1894, had formed both of these.

The 1894 Act had also divided the local government of Cannock between separate Urban District and Rural District councils, the former having responsibility for the town itself; the latter for that of its outlying districts. In its early days the clerk to Cannock RDC was based in the town itself, whilst the Medical Officer was in Cheslyn Hay and the Sanitary Inspector & Surveyor was based in Penkridge. The area governed was part of a broader Cannock Union, and as such made use of the Workhouse in the town, which was built in 1872. In the early 20th century Cannock RDC began to hold alternate meetings in the Littleton Arms in Penkridge, before finding a permanent home in the Haling Dene Centre, where Penkridge Parish Council currently has their offices.

Seisdon was perhaps an odd choice to head a Rural District, but the origins of this rested with the creation of a Poor Law Union on 17 October 1836, based around the Seisdon Hundred. This built a workhouse in Trysull in 1859, in whose boardroom the council held its fortnightly meetings. However, despite having this base, all of the council's main officers lived in Wolverhampton. With the closure of the workhouse in 1930 the authority moved to an old residence on Gravel Hill in Wombourne, near to which new purpose-built offices were opened on 29 April 1968.

The areas governed by both RDC's were 'fine-tuned' by successive generations of Local Government Acts, notably those in 1900 and 1966. The Staffordshire Review Order, 1934, resulted in further boundary changes, which made numerous minor alterations to parish boundaries and exchanged parishes, and parts thereof, both within what would eventually become South Staffordshire, and between adjoining areas, such as Stafford, Cannock and Wolverhampton.

The boundary between Cannock Rural District Council and Seisdon Rural District Council ran just south of Chillington Hall, Gunstone, Coven Heath, Featherstone, Essington and Newtown, and today is more or less the line of the M54.

At first glance, the nature of the former RDC areas may seem very different. The northern former Cannock part is sometimes characterised as being less developed, with large tracts of land in the east being given over to mining. Whilst this may be true, this same half of the present district has by far the greater proportion of listed buildings – 57% to 43% – and 80% of the Grade I listed buildings. Another misconception is that all of the former industry was in the north of the district. Again, this is untrue. Seisdon RDC was home to a number of quarries, several large iron and steelworks, plus at least one major colliery at Baggeridge.

South Staffordshire's development owes much to the many interlocking landed estates that, historically, formed around half of its area. Estate control and patronage also literally imposed a house-style on many of the buildings erected before the 20th century.

Change was gradual, and came in waves. First came the canals. South Staffordshire is lucky in having sizeable portions of two very significant canal lines cutting through it. The Staffordshire & Worcestershire Canal was fully opened on 28 May 1772. It was the only main line canal to be completed by the legendary engineer James Brindley, and, at Wombourne, featured both the first lock and first lock flight built on a canal in the UK. Two generations later the Birmingham & Liverpool Canal (now the Shropshire Union) also cut through the district, mostly in a straight line. It opened on 2 March 1835, and is acknowledged as the finest canal work by Thomas Telford.

Two years later, on 4 July 1837, the Grand Junction Railway opened. It was the first trunk railway in the country, and runs parallel to the A449, with a station at Penkridge. Railways brought goods, passengers, trade, and, most of all an ever increasing pace of change. The Shrewsbury & Birmingham Railway opened on 12 November 1849, and crossed South Staffordshire between Oaken and Bilbrook. There was a station at Codsall, which was joined by another at Bilbrook in 1934. The line's construction required the opening up of quarries around Histons Hill, the surplus stone from which can be seen in walls and houses throughout the area. The railway itself became caught up in rivalry between the two largest railway companies to reach Birmingham, and was quickly swallowed up by the Great Western. Snaking through the southern part of the district is the South Staffordshire Railway Walk, formed along the track bed of the former Great Western Railway Stourbridge-Wolverhampton line, which was begun in 1913 but only completed in 1925. Between 11 May 1925 and 31 October 1932 a passenger service operated along this line – one of the last to be built in the country – serving stations at Himley, Wombourne and Penn.

The combined effect of the railways, buses, and trams serving Wolverhampton and Kinver, was to open up South Staffordshire to day-trippers, some of whom liked the places they visited so much that they bought or built houses there. Forming a rural fringe to the Birmingham and Black Country conurbations, these visitors were also faced with wide choice of open spaces, tea- rooms and gardens, and hostelries in places such as Kinver, Enville, Penn, Trysull, Codsall and Shoal Hill. Later, from the 1960s onwards, when private cars made the prospect of residing in rural areas and commuting to work a practical proposition, large housing estates were developed in many areas. Despite this, South Staffordshire remains predominantly a rural area.

This is the nature of South Staffordshire Council's inheritance, and the essence of what the authority has sought to preserve and enhance during the last 30 years. In celebration, this book takes the form of a meandering perambulation down the district, from north to south. All 27 parishes are visited in turn. If history is a journey – does anyone fancy a walk?

DUNSTON with COPPENHALL

Dunston

The name is derived from the Anglo-Saxon for 'Dunn's Farmstead.' Dunston is 2 miles north of Penkridge and 3 miles south of Stafford. The parish was formed in 1844 out of Penkridge and includes the neighbouring hamlet of Dunston Heath. Dunston Hall was formerly the home of the Thorneycroft family. The local economy was wholly devoted to agriculture and in 1933 the County Council bought 103 acres there, establishing eight smallholdings, each with its own house. The church, dedicated to St Leonard, was erected between 1876 and 1878, on the site of an earlier building, which had early 15th century origins. The new church was built at the expense of Frederick Perry and his family in memory of his father, Thomas Perry, who died in 1861. A school was built in 1866 and enlarged in 1910.

Nikolaus Pevsner described the **Church of St Leonard**, Dunston as: *'a large church of the estate type, i.e. a town church in the country.'* The Perry family rebuilt it into its present form in 1876-8 at a cost of £5,000 in memory of Thomas Perry. A cruciform stone building in the Early Decorated style, its spire contains 8 bells and a clock, all the gift of Miss Perry. The burial ground was added to the churchyard in 1887, a new vestry added in 1906, and a new organ installed.

Coppenhall

Coppenhall village stands on an eminence, 3 miles southwest from Stafford and 4 miles northwest from Penkridge. The name is derived from the Anglo-Saxon for 'Coppa's Nook of Land.' Recorded in Domesday, the village was formerly wholly dependent upon agriculture, and was unusual in lacking an overall landowner, most of the land belonging to individual farmers. Being in a prominent position, Coppenhall was once the site of two windmills, the first of which stood, appropriately enough, in Windmill Field, adjoining Hyde Lea, the second of which, standing west of Butterhill Farm, worked until the 1870s, and did not have its tackle removed until 1912. This also had the distinction of being the only six-sail windmill in Staffordshire. The church, dedicated to St Lawrence, has its origins in the 12th century, and is unusual in that it survives in a relatively unaltered state.

The Church of St. Lawrence, Coppenhall, which Nikolaus Pevsner described as: *'a perfect 13th century village church, small but of great dignity'*, was restored... It was restored and re-roofed in 1866, but this did not alter the basic form of the original church. The timber-framed bell cote is 16th century, and was also restored in 1866. The earliest entry in the Register of Baptisms is from 13th January 1678; the earliest marriage recorded being in 1684. Burials were not made in the churchyard until 1871, the ground not being consecrated until 1870; the first entry in the Register of Burials being for 20th January 1871.

Left: ***Dunston Hall*** is first mentioned in a conveyance of land in 1607, but the present building, seen here, was not built until the mid-19th century. It is a fine example of the then popular Italianate style of architecture. For many years it was the home of the Perry family, who funded the rebuilding of the nearby Church of St Leonard between 1876-8 in memory of Thomas Perry. Passing to the Thorneycroft family in 1900, the Hall was sold and converted to flats in 1951, but sold on to English Electric as offices in 1956. For a number of years the Hall was also the head office of Leigh Environmental.

Right: ***Pool Farm***, on the main A449 at Dunston, is a good example of an Estate building. The many landed estates, which make up a sizeable portion of South Staffordshire, each had a house-style of building, which, once appreciated, lends great character to its villages. Pool Farm was once part of the Thorneycroft Estate, whose ownership is declared by the square tablet on the chimney, which bears their armorial device.

Left: ***Butterhill Farm windmill*** stood approximately 100 yards northwest of Butterhill Farmhouse and worked until the 1870s. It was the only six-sail windmill in Staffordshire, and its remaining tackle was removed in 1912. Like many other examples in South Staffordshire, its solidly built tower has proven much more durable, and still stands. It is also a listed structure, none of which seems to be troubling these cows too much.

ACTON TRUSSELL, BEDNALL AND TEDDESLEY HAY

Acton Trussell

Acton Trussell is 2½ miles northeast from Penkridge and 3½ miles southeast from Stafford. It is mentioned in Domesday: *'the Bishop of Chester holds Actone (Acton). Robert holds it from him. [... hides] Land for 4 ploughs. In lordship 1; 10 villagers and 8 smallholders with 4 ploughs. A mill at 2s; meadow, 8 acres; woodland 3 furlongs long and 2 furlongs wide. Value before 1066, 5s; now 20s.'* The name Acton is derived from the Saxon words ac-tun meaning 'oak-tree farmstead.' In order to eliminate confusion Norman administrators introduced the practice of manorial suffixes, whereby the name of the predominant family was affixed to the common place-name. So by 1481 the settlement was named Acton Trussel after the Trussel family, who are named in manorial records from 1342. In May 1985 the semi hexagonal wing of a Roman villa was discovered south of Acton Trussell. Ongoing excavations have shown this to be 4th century with 1st century origins.

Bednall

Bednall is 3½ miles northeast from Penkridge and 4½ miles southeast from Stafford. It is mentioned in Domesday: *'the Bishop of Chester holds Broctone (Brocton) and Bedehala (Bednall). They belong to BERCHESVVIC (Baswich) and are waste.'* The village was wholly devoted to agriculture; the stiff clay soil being particularly suited for the growing of barley, clover, oats, seeds, turnips and wheat. The Staffordshire Way, a long distance footpath running for 93 miles from Mow Cop on the Staffordshire/Cheshire border to Kinver Edge on the Staffordshire and Worcestershire border, passes through Bednall. The Staffordshire & Worcestershire Canal, the only canal wholly completed by James Brindley, runs to the east of the village, and the towpath and the network of local footpaths give a variety of local walks. The Teddesley Boat Company provides a canal boat hire facility nearby.

Teddesley Hay

Teddesley Hay is a parish, about 2¾ miles northeast from Penkridge, and 5 miles from Stafford. It was a division of the royal forest of Cannock from before 1100, and remained unenclosed until 1820. The area was transformed during the lifetime of Edward John, 1st Baron Hatherton, who brought the area into a high state of cultivation and had substantial farm buildings and cottages erected before his death in 1863. A mediaeval house stood on a moated site, which lay 200 yards northwest of Teddesley Hall, a large mansion house built by Sir Edward Littleton, c.1750, with the proceeds from two hoards of coins found behind panelling at Pillaton Hall in 1742 and 1749. Teddesley Hall was unoccupied following the death of the 3rd Lord Hatherton in 1930. Used by troops and for prisoners of war during World War II, it subsequently stood empty and was demolished in 1954.

*Left: **The Moat House** in Acton Trussell stands on the site of a mediaeval moated manor house. It has been rebuilt and altered many times over the years, the greatest part of the present building dating from the early 16th century. Originally wholly timber-framed, the first brick-built elements were added in the early 18th century, and much of its exterior was subsequently brick-faced. The building is seen here in 1979, before its conversion into a prestigious hotel and restaurant.*

Right: North east of the Moat House is **The Old School House**, a late 16th century timber-framed building that, despite its name, was not used for formal education but was used as a Sunday School in the 19th and 20th centuries. The house was remodelled in the mid-19th century to make the southwest side of its cross wing into the front entrance; this *'turning round'* of houses being quite commonly seen in the district.

Left: Just south west of the Old Schoolhouse stands this mill barn. The single-storey building attached to the chimney houses a boiler and steam engine, which powered milling equipment within the main barn. All of this equipment remains, making these buildings: *'a complete example of a formerly steam driven mill barn of which few examples remain in western lowland Staffordshire'*, according to J E C Peters authoritative account on the subject, published in 1969.

Right: At the north of Acton Trussell village are the Old Homage and Old Croft cottage, seen here. Both are 16th century, timber-framed, and thatched, although the framing has been faced with brick. They stand as testimony to the age and importance of Acton Trussell as a settlement.

Above: The Staffordshire & Worcestershire Canal runs north to the west of Acton Trussell. **Acton Moat Bridge** is No.92 on the line, and carries Mill Lane out of the village towards Acton Gate. Despite having been repaired and strengthened over the years, the bridge retains much of its original fabric.

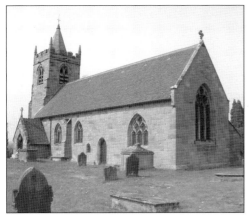

Left: The **Church of St James**, Acton Trussell, was originally a chapel-of-ease to Baswich and only became a parish church after the Reformation. Its oldest portions – the eastern two-thirds of the single chamber – are 14th century, possibly dating from as early as c.1300, which is also the date of the tower, although the top and recessed spire date from 1562. The church was restored in 1869-70 by G.E. Street, RA, at which time the western part and the north chapel were rebuilt and the porch added.

Right: The **Church of All Saints**, Bednall, was built of stone in the Early English style between 1843 and 1846, to replace an older building which stood further back from the road. This was last used in June 1843; the foundation stone of the new church being laid on 17th February 1845. All Saints was consecrated on 10th August 1846. In memory of their mother, Mary Heath of Bednall Hall and her sister Anne Stokes added an east window in 1864. Both the tower and spire were added in 1873, again the gift of Mary Heath, and she and her sister also gave, respectively, a single bell and a clock.

Above: William White's Directory of Staffordshire (1851) noted that: *'Sir Edward Littleton … erected Teddesley Hall, a noble mansion, seated on an eminence, two and a quarter miles NE of Penkridge, nearly in the centre of this now fertile liberty, a large portion of which forms the park, pleasure grounds, and gardens, and the rest is a large highly cultivated farm of 1700 acres, in the occupation of the owner, Lord Hatherton, who resides at the Hall.'* Sadly, the main hall was demolished in 1954, but many of the service blocks remain, and plans exist to rebuild the original house in close to its original form.

BLYMILL AND WESTON-UNDER-LIZARD

Blymill

Blymhill stands 6 miles northeast from Shifnal and 6 miles northwest from Brewood. Slightly northeast from Weston-under-Lizard, Blymhill formed part of the Earl of Bradford's estate and once housed workers from the estate. It contains a number of fine listed buildings. The church is dedicated to St Mary and has 14th century origins. Despite being extensively rebuilt it retains many original features. Under the terms of the Staffordshire Review Order, 1934, parts of the adjoining parishes of Church Eaton and Gnosall were added to Blymhill.

Weston-under-Lizard

Weston-under-Lizard is a model village standing on Watling Street, 6 miles northwest of Brewood. The 'Lizard' is a hill, 2¹/₂ miles to the southwest and 480 feet in height. The whole village belongs to the Earl of Bradford (head of the Bridgemen family). The Hall, a palatial residence, was built by Sir Thomas Wilbraham in 1671 and occupies the site of an ancient manor house, which was in the possession of the de Weston family until 1340. A memorial to one of them, Sir John de Weston and his wife, was incorporated (in the form of kneeling figures) in the 14th century east window of the church, together with their coat-of-arms. Weston Hall is also a possible location for the fictional Blandings Castle in P G Wodehouse's novels.

A church, dedicated to St Andrew, stands in the park. This has 12th century origins but was rebuilt in 1700-01, and restored in 1876. There are a number of interesting features inside, including a carved oak pulpit, with brass sounding board, dating from 1702 – the year the Church was substantially rebuilt by Lady Wilbraham. The Perpendicular tower (not rebuilt) contains three bells of pre-Reformation date, two of them being inscribed with the legend 'Hail, Mary!' A school was opened in 1873, but private education had been available for at least 40 years beforehand, some of which was supported by the Earl of Bradford. Four almshouses were also built at the expense of Selina, Countess of Bradford, in 1874 for the poor of the parish.

Weston Park is open to the public and plays host to a series of weekend events each year between March and November, of which the 'V' music festival, held each August, is probably the most famous. The gardens at Weston Park are a good example of an 18th century landscape garden where Capability Brown once worked. The woodland garden has a fine collection of trees, rhododendrons and azaleas with pathways and ponds. The formal gardens include a 19th century Italian Parterre. There is also a Rose walk, which leads to the Deer Park.

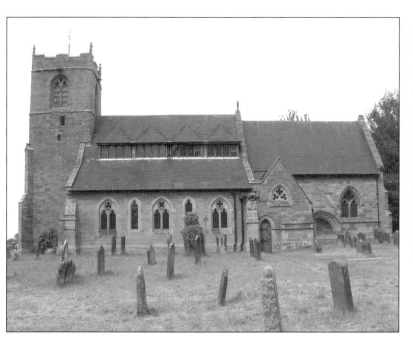

Left: **The Church of St. Mary**, Blymhill, has its origins in the mid-14th century, the register dating from 1561. It was extensively restored and enlarged between 1856-9 to designs by G E Street, at a cost of £3,800. The School, also by Street, was built between 1855-7, as was a Rectory. The Dickenson family had a long association with the church, three of whom were rectors of the parish. St Mary's contains a number of memorials to various Dickensons, including the Rev. Samuel Dickenson, a noted botanist, who died on 15 May 1823.

Above: Blymhill was home to many workers on the Earl of Bradford's estate, many of whom lived in simple cottages like this one. Of 18th century origin, the upper storey had no ceiling as such, headroom being afforded by the roof space.

Above: Many of the cottages in Blymhill are of some considerable age. The Black & White Cottage, seen here centre left, is 17th century, with later alterations and additions, which included a brick built extension to the right in the 19th century. Originally, the cottage would have been thatched.

Above: There was a school in Blymhill from the late 17th century courtesy of the will of the Rev. John Taylor. The National system of teaching was adopted in 1834, and the buildings seen here replaced the original ones in 1856.

Above: **Great Chatwell** is part of Blymhill parish. The aptly-named Brick Kiln Cottage is of mid-19th century origin, and is unusual in that it stands next to a brick kiln, seen here centre right. This does not appear to have been worked commercially, and therefore may have supplied a local estate. When photographed in 1979 the kiln had been long out of use, and its flue much reduced in height.

Right: **Weston Hall** stands within its own parkland, some of which is outside the district. The original building dates from the 1670s, with the design being attributed to Lady Wilbraham, but the Hall seen today owes much to alterations and additions of the early-, mid- and late - 19th century. Like a number of other large houses, the entrance to Weston Hall has been moved, in this case from the South to the East front. Weston Park is widely used as a venue for many outdoor events, of which the annual 'V' music festivals each August are the most widely known.

PENKRIDGE

Penkridge boasts a long history, being situated close to the site of Penncrucium (now known as Stretton), a Roman station, and only 2 miles from the Roman Watling Street. The place also had some importance in Saxon days. A Roman camp was discovered at Engleton, about three miles from Penkridge, which derives its name from a Celtic word meaning *'the end of the boundary.'*

Penkridge is situated on the main Wolverhampton-Stafford road and still has a rural aspect, heightened by the asset of the River Penk flowing through it. The village is also served by rail, having a station on the former Grand Junction Railway, the first trunk line built in the country, which opened on 4 July 1837. It was once famous for its horse fair, but retains a popular open market held every Wednesday and Saturday. The village has a rich collection of historic buildings, many of which are timber framed in origin and at heart. Some have a good tale to tell, such as the library in Bellbrook, which began as the Penkridge Savings' Bank in 1819, but, after failing spectacularly, became a police station in 1858, and retains its cellblock today.

Visitors are well catered for at Penkridge's various hotels and inns – one of which, The White Hart, is of ancient lineage and according to legend, once entertained Elizabeth I when she passed through the district. Another interesting hostelry is the Littleton Arms, named after the Littleton family of nearby Pillaton Old Hall.

The parish church is dedicated to St. Michael and All Angels. It was formerly St. Mary's, one of the six Collegiate Churches in Staffordshire, and had a Dean and four Prebendaries. There was a church on the same site in the reign of King Stephen, and the original foundation is believed to date from 850. It is mentioned as St. Mary's Church in the Close Rolls of Henry III. Towards the end of the 19th century, extensive restoration and improvements were carried out, including the lowering of the Nave floor to its original level. Parts of the ancient walls are incorporated in the present building, which is a fine example of the Perpendicular style. The interior presents a noble aspect with its clerestoried Chancel and clerestoried Nave, having four bays, the pillars and capitals being of a particularly simple dignity. An especially noteworthy feature is the wrought-iron screen of Dutch workmanship executed in 1778. The village War Memorial, designed by Sir Charles Nicholson, is inserted in the churchyard wall.

Some houses of note distinguish Penkridge, including Pillaton Old Hall, which originally dated from the 15th century, some of which has been preserved, notably the Chapel, dedicated to St Modwena. The Chapel was built in 1488 in memory of Richard Littleton and his wife, Alice. It was restored in 1888. Pillaton Old Hall was originally guarded by a moat, which still remains to add picturesque interest to the buildings. Rodbaston Hall, a large redbrick mansion with a 300-acre farm is now a noted Agricultural College. There is a noteworthy row of Almshouses, of Elizabethan design, which were erected by the Dowager Lady Hatherton in 1866 as a memorial to the first Lord Hatherton.

Above: **Crown Bridge**, Penkridge, looking from the main A449 about 1980. In the mid-18th century there was a bridge and a ford across the Boscomoor (known locally as 'Boosmoore') Brook at this point – hence the name. In the same period, the large formally planted area to the centre left was also occupied by buildings.

Above: Looking towards Dunston from the tower of St Michael & All Angels in Penkridge about a century ago. The houses in the foreground are in Pinfold Lane, and the land immediately behind them is now occupied by Penkridge's market. The Penk flows across the centre of the picture, passing beneath Stone Cross Bridge, which carries the road now known as the A449 away towards Stafford. To the left of the bridge, mansions in Levedale Road can be glimpsed through the trees.
Lyndsey Edwards

Above: Few buildings in Penkridge have had a more interesting past than the current library. Built as a Savings' Bank in 1819, the building was converted to a Police Station in 1858, but was superseded in this role by new buildings erected in 1954. The main building interior was largely gutted by this last conversion, but the brick-built cellblock to left rear, dating from 1858, retains its original cells. These are gems, and retain all their original fixtures and fittings.

Above: Land at Pillaton belonged to Burton Abbey until the dissolution, when it passed to the Paget family. It can be assumed that there was a hall at Pillaton at this time, but the present buildings there, seen here, date from the 16th century. The site was moated (drained in 1860) and this view shows the bridge over the moat, plus the gatehouse range. At the eastern end of this is a chapel dedicated to St Modwena, and the range to view here is the remaining north side of a quadrangle, which formerly surrounded an inner courtyard.

Left: In operation, canals are wasteful of water, and require 'topping up.' Where a natural watercourse could be tapped, it was. Generally though maintaining a working level on a canal required the construction of a reservoir. The Staffordshire & Worcestershire Canal has one such at Gailey, alongside the A5. This derelict pump house there formerly maintained the level of the reservoir.

Right: **The Church of St Michael and All Angels**, Penkridge, is the largest parish church in South Staffordshire. Its construction started in the 12th century and was completed in the 14th century, with later alterations and additions. Perpendicular in style, there are now no traces of earlier Saxon or Norman churches. Successive work throughout the ages has wrought changes and there is a fine new late 20th century screen in the tower. The bell ropes here are some of the longest in England, providing a challenge to any bell ringer.

Above and Right: At the heart of **The White Hart** on Stone Cross in Penkridge is an early 17th century house, which has been restored, and whose façade was substantially rebuilt in the early 20th century. Despite this, it retains the appearance of an earlier coaching inn; the entrance beneath, to the right in this view, remains cobbled to this day and formerly lead to stabling behind. At right is an advert for The White Hart from the late 1950s, which shows very little change to the current view.

THE WHITE HART

BEST BUTLER'S ALES AND STOUTS

on main

WOLVERHAMPTON-STAFFORD ROAD

SNACKS · CAR PARK

LIGHT REFRESHMENTS

FULLY LICENSED
— PROP.: H M. LYONS —

Tel. Penkridge 242

Above and Right: **The Littleton Arms** at the corner of St Michael's Square and Clay Street, Penkridge, is named in honour of the family which owner a number of the estates comprising or adjoining the village, including Pillaton and Preston. Of early 19th century construction, the building is seen above in the early 1980s and right in an advert from the late 1950s. On a main road, and close to the railway, the pub has always been well located to do good business.

"LITTLETON ARMS"
PENKRIDGE
BEST BUTLER ALES & STOUTS

Coach Parties Welcome
Large free Car Park

o

SNACKS — PARTIES
ACCOMMODATED

o

Telephone: 287
Prop. A. W. PROSSER

on main
STAFFORD–WOLVERHAMPTON ROAD

Left: **Bellbrook** links Mill Street and Cannock Road in Penkridge. In addition to a school and the village Library, it also has a few buildings of a considerable age, including the Lock-up and, here, the Old Cottage. This is of 15th century origin, with 17th century alterations and 20th century fenestration. In the years since this view was taken, the Morris Oxford parked in front has become quite a period piece in itself!

Below: **Market Street,** Penkridge links the Market Place with the main A449. Now one way, owing to its narrowness, for at least 400 years buildings have delineated both the street and place. The age of some of these buildings is evident in this view from the early 1980s, and even the brick faced ones reveal timber-framed interiors upon closer examination.

Right: The outlying hamlet of Whiston is part of Penkridge Parish. **Whiston Mill,** seen here in 1964, dates from at least 1370, when it is first recorded. The Giffard family of Chillington Hall owned the mill until 1841, from whence it was worked by a succession of millers until 1928. The mill house continued to be lived in and was extended between the late 1960s and early 1980s, but the mill remained relatively untouched. As a result, on 18 June 2004 it became the district's most recently listed building.

Right and Above: The point at which the Staffordshire & Worcestershire Canal intersected the A5 at Gailey was destined to be an important transhipment point, and it is not surprising that a wharf for this purpose was constructed there. The area is a busy one for the canal, as, in addition to the wharf, there is also lock at this point, seen *above*. Lockkeeper's houses were traditionally built tall to afford uninterrupted views across long lines of canal. For obvious reasons, the one at Gailey *(right)* is known as **The Round House**, and it makes a singular and distinctive contribution to the scene there.

HUNTINGTON

Huntington is a mile north of Cannock and formed part of the lands held by the Littleton family. It was wood and common land, which, in 1665, had a small hamlet supporting just 46 families. They had extensive rights of pasture over Huntington Common and Huntington Heath, but these were extinguished by enclosure in 1827. There were few buildings too: some cottages at the north end, and a chantry chapel, which predated the Reformation. During this time the population grew slowly, and by 1801 only 114 people were recorded.

This slow pace of growth continued throughout the 19th century. A Wesleyan Chapel was built in 1847, and the church of St Thomas, with a school, was built in 1872 to designs by Edward Richards, and was enlarged in 1879. At the same time, the South Staffordshire Waterworks Company built a pumping station at Huntington, which was completed in 1877. It was designed by Henry Naden of Birmingham and built by William Trow & Sons of Wednesbury, and housed a pair of steam engines.

Apart from farming, the only industry was the extraction and distribution of white gravel, used in vast quantities to cover paths and drives. The whole character of the area was changed completely from 1899 when the West Cannock Colliery Company sank a successful mine, and thereafter miners flocked in. By 1931 Huntington's population had increased fivefold, from 351 in 1901, to 1,816. This influx required additional schools: in 1921 a Public Elementary School was established, and in 1934 responsibility for the church school was transferred to the County Council.

Up to and during the Second World War mining continued to prosper, and modern pit head baths were erected in 1939, and completed in 1941. After the war there was a downturn in the mining industry, and this, combined with increasing subsidence problems, put a halt on Huntington's further growth. The 1951 census showed that its population, recorded as 1,587, had begun to decline, and, mainly as a result of this, the development of a large council housing estate was deferred until 1959.

Huntington Pumping Station remained a prominent local landmark. It was modernised in 1937, when electrically driven pumps replaced the steam engines, and much of the paraphernalia associated with steam working was removed. Superseded by a modern installation built nearby in Limepit Lane, the pumping station was decommissioned in 1981, and, despite being listed on 8 May that year, it fell prey to vandalism that was so extensive that the building had to be demolished in January 1984. The site is now occupied by a housing association development.

Huntington Colliery seemed to weather all of the vicissitudes of the mining industry during the 1980s, and appeared to have a secure future, but it too eventually succumbed, closing on 9 December 1993.

Left: The South Staffordshire Water Works Co. built a pumping station at Huntington in 1877. It was designed by Henry Naden of Birmingham, built by William Trow & Sons of Wednesbury, and once housed a pair of steam engines. Unusually, the ends of the beams bearing the pump rods protruded from the side of the building, as seen here, and each bore an elaborate fluted-sided, dome-topped counterweight.

Left: Huntington pumping station was modernised in 1937. Electrically driven pumps replaced the steam engines, and much of the paraphernalia associated with steam working was removed. In addition, two modern flat-roofed wings were added, but the elaborately decorated octagonal-sided chimney remained.

Left: By early-1981 Huntington pumping station was nearing the end of its working life. South Staffordshire Water was building a replacement facility nearby in Limepit Lane. This photograph dates from that year, and shows that by this time the chimney had also been demolished. An air raid siren sits on top of the flat-roof (centre left). Utility buildings like this were often used as anti-aircraft observation posts and were protected by Home Guard Units.

Left: Upon its closure, South Staffordshire Water announced its intention to demolish Huntington Pumping Station. Upon learning of this South Staffordshire Council applied to the Department of the Environment to have the building, and its associated cottages, listed. On 8 May 1981 the pumping station alone was listed Grade II. Huntington Pumping Station was demolished in January 1984, a very sad loss to the District.

Below: **Littleton Colliery** at Huntington was the last to work on the South Staffordshire coalfield. This is a reminder of its final days when it was part of the National Coal Board. Today, the perimeter fence, seen in the foreground, is all that remains from the once massive pit complex.

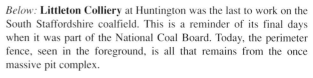

Left: Above ground Littleton Colliery was a magnet for steam enthusiasts, as it was one of the last pits in the country to retain steam locomotives for the internal movement of coal around the site. The photographs at left were all taken on 10 April 1976, and are very evocative of a rapidly dying industry and transport system. The smoke plumes are especially impressive – what were they burning on those locos? *Geoff Cryer/www.geoffspages.co.uk*

Below: a single line leads off to the main colliery buildings.

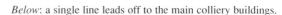

Above: This row of miners' cottages, with their characteristically tall chimneys, have outlasted Littleton Colliery. The large structure dominating the background was the focal point for the various conveyor systems bringing coal from below ground.

Right: Littleton Colliery closed on 9 December 1993, and the surface buildings were gradually dismantled over the following months. As at many other former pits, a headstock wheel was set up as a memorial to the colliery. This can be seen in this view of the site, taken in October 1994. The skeletal form of the conveyor system centre building dominates the background.

LAPLEY, STRETTON AND WHEATON ASTON

Lapley

Lapley is about 4 miles from Brewood. It once had a Priory of Black Monks, which was bestowed on the Abbey of Saint Remigius at Rhiems during the reign of Edward the Confessor. Lerfric, Earl of Mercia, married to Lady Godiva, had a young grandson, Burchard, who went to Rome with the Archbishop of Canterbury on a mission. On their return Burchard was taken ill and died at Rheims in France. He told the monks if they allowed him to be buried there, his father would give them lands and a church in England. His request was granted and Lapley was given to the monks who built the priory.

This suffered the fate of most alien priories in the reign of Henry I, and it became the property of the college of Tong in Shropshire, but Henry V suppressed it. During the civil war the Priory House was fortified and garrisoned for the King, under the command of Captain Smith; but in 1645 Cromwell's troops took it and made the people round pay to have the fortifications taken away. Under a Parliamentary order every constable within the liberties of Aston, Bradley, Bickford, Lapley, Marston, Mitton, Stretton and Whiston was commanded to attend with six men each and forthwith: *'pull down the works and fortifications around Lapley Church.'*

Captain Smith is buried in the chancel of All Saints Church, an ancient priory church, whose register dates from 1538 and which retains some Norman portions. Cruciform in shape, the nave or body of the Church is not directly at right angles to the Altar. In times past malcontents were punished by being placed at the back of the Church, from where the Altar could not be seen.

Under the Staffordshire Review Order of 1934 Lapley's boundaries were changed: part of it was transferred to Penkridge, and parts of Bradley and Penkridge were added to Lapley.

Stretton

Stretton consists of a small-scattered hamlet situated on the Watling Street and equidistant from both Stafford and Wolverhampton. It centres round Stretton Hall, which is now the seat of the Monckton family, but which was originally built for a Connolly by Inigo Jones in 1620. It contains the best known example of a hanging staircase, i.e. one hung from the roof on chains, of which only one other example can be found in England, viz., at Norwich, and still has a central fireplace with steps up it for a boy to be sent up to sweep it! It was at one time the home of the Congreve family, including the poet William Congreve (1670-1729), who is commemorated by an oak tree bearing his name. He was responsible for many lines still used or paraphrased today, including: *'Music hath charms to soothe a savage breast,'* and *'Heaven has no rage like love so hatred turned, Nor hell a fury like a woman scorned.'*

Stretton Church is of very early origin, the Chancel that still contains a fixed stone altar (which was made illegal at the time of the reformation) and a stone shell, which shewed that its owner had been on a Crusade, dates back to the 12th century. The Nave of the Church has twice been demolished by fire. Originally a Chapel of Ease of Penkridge, Stretton subsequently became a separate parish and is now held in plurality with Penkridge. The Church is built of stone and dedicated to St. John.

Stretton Pool was constructed over some springs at the expense of Mrs A Monckton around 1860 in order to wipe out malaria, which was then infecting the whole village. Sadly, the drainers all caught the disease and became prematurely aged, most of them dying comparatively young.

A striking feature is an iron aqueduct, built by Thomas Telford in 1832, which carries the Shropshire Union Canal over the A5.

Wheaton Aston

Wheaton Aston is a village about 1½ miles west of Lapley. It contains a number of interesting timber-framed houses, and is famous as the most northerly point where Fritillaria Meleagris – the Snakes Head Fritillary – is found growing in the wild. This local interest is reflected in a mosaic of the plant incorporated into the District Council's Environmental Improvement Scheme around the church and the village centre. Wheaton Aston was devastated by a fire on 9 April 1777, which destroyed 19 houses, 16 outhouses, and caused damage estimated at in excess of £2,030. The church, dedicated to St Mary, was built in 1857 to designs by the Wolverhampton architects Bidlake & Lovatt. It replaced a chapel dedicated to the Holy Trinity which had 14th century origins. A Primitive Methodist Chapel was built in 1832, and a National School was erected in 1853-4, which took over the duties of a schoolmaster whose post had been funded by a bequest in 1702. There is also a Reading Room, which was built in 1886-7, and a Memorial Hall, built in 1927 to the memory of Molly Owen, late President of the local Women's Institute.

Left: Old fingerpost signs in timber and cast-iron lend great character to many of South Staffordshire's villages. This example is on Long Street, Wheaton Aston, close to the Shropshire Union Canal, and very neatly introduces this section of the book.

Left: Lapley is centred on a small knot of roads, which focus upon a triangular green. Approaching Lapley along Bickford Road, with the **Vaughn Arms** on the right, about 1981. A late-model Austin Maxi is parked partly on the grass verge of the green, next to the phone box. Whilst previous generations may have thought modern street furniture a visual intrusion, today, phone boxes, fingerposts and the like add greatly to the charm of village centres such as Lapley.

Right: **The Church of All Saints**, Lapley, was originally a church to a small priory, founded just after the Norman Conquest as a dependency of an abbey in France. The chancel retains one original south window, and was extended by one bay in the 13th century. In 1414, whilst Henry V was at war with France, an Act of Parliament was passed dissolving the priory. In its original form the church was cruciform, but only the nave, central tower and chancel remain from this today. The register dates from 1538. The church was repaired in 1857. In 1929 the original sanctus bell, then one of only three ancient bells of this kind left in the country, was re-hung in the chancel.

Left: **The Old Vicarage** in Lapley was built in the late 18th century. Unusually, it is not immediately next to the church, but a small distance off to the northeast. The building was altered in the 19th century by the addition of a bay to left of the entrance.

Left: Thomas Telford's canal crosses the main A5 at Stretton, and is carried across by this elegant cast-iron aqueduct. The inscription reads: *'Birmingham and Liverpool Canal Thos. Telford FRSI&E Engineer 1832'*, this being the line's original title. To give greater headroom, in the 20th century the roadway was lowered, requiring the construction of the blue brick plinths to the abutments, which can be seen peering out from the grass.

Right: Just north of the aqueduct there is a wharf on the **Shropshire Union Canal** at Stretton, which is a popular mooring place. An added attraction there is a small boat repair yard. With its traditional boats, this view has a timeless quality which belies the fact that it was taken on 13 July 2004.

Below: **Stretton Mill** is one of a number of former watermills in the district that retain much of their equipment. Of early 19th century construction, Stretton Mill retains the cast-iron hoops to the mills undershot gable wall mounted wheel, plus two grindstone cases on the first floor, with inset plaques bearing the legend *'Kay & Hilton, Fleet Street, Liverpool 1854.'* Other equipment remaining includes the grinding axle, mill gear and grain storage bins.

Left: The Millennium made people in villages up and down the country think of ways in which to mark this important milestone. In Wheaton Aston a square was laid out *(see below)*, and as part of the Carnival held in the village on 3 July 2004, a time capsule was buried in this. The spot is marked by this stone, which gives precise instructions that the capsule is to be opened exactly 50 years after it was buried.

Right: The **Church of St. Mary**, Wheaton Aston, had its origins in the 17th century as a Chapel of Ease. It was rebuilt in 1857 to the designs of the Wolverhampton Architects Bidlake & Lovatt. Repairs followed in 1882, and a stone chancel, by C. Lynam, was added in 1893, fitted with a carved oak screen and choir stalls. More recently, the church, photographed here in 1969, was floodlit via grant aid from the Countryside Agency's Rural Recovery Programme.

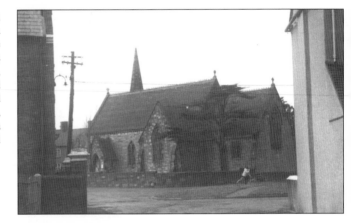

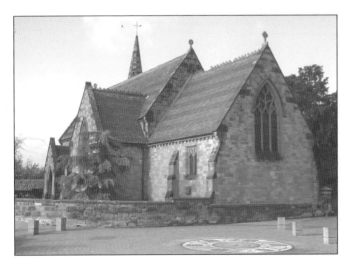

Left: The **Church of St. Mary,** Wheaton Aston, in 2004, with its Millennium Square seen centre right in the foreground.

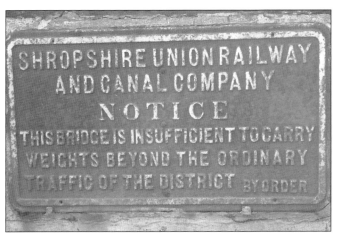

Left: In the midst of the Railway Mania, in the early 1840s, a number of railway proposals and canal interests were pooled to form the Shropshire Union Railway and Canal Company, part of whose scheme was to turn some canals into railways. As a venture it did not get too far, but the name stuck, albeit with the dropping of the *'Railway And'* from the company name. This bridge plate is on one of the roadside parapet walls of Tavern Bridge in Long Street, Wheaton Aston.

Right: The stretch of the Shropshire Union Canal south of Tavern Bridge is another popular mooring point, where British Waterways has provided watering and sanitary facilities. Tavern Bridge can be seen right rear in this view.

Left: Today the lock at Wheaton Aston is a little more overgrown than in this early 20th century view. Also, the pair of cottages have been demolished, but the Telford-designed tollhouse to the left remains, divorced from the canal by a fence and hedge. All of Telford's tollhouses, whether for his roads or canals, were of a basic design.

HATHERTON

Bisected by the old Roman road known as Watling Street, now the A5, Hatherton extends from Shoal Hill in the northeast to Four Ashes in the southwest. The village of Hatherton lies on the southern slope of Shoal Hill, which was for many years a popular resort for local people, and for tourists from Cannock and the Black Country. Hatherton was amongst the lands seized by William Wallhouse during the reign of James I. His descendant, Moreton Wallhouse, rebuilt Hatherton Hall in stone in 1817, adopting the Gothic style. The church of St Saviour was built in 1864, redecorated twice, in 1876 and 1887, and renovated in 1923, works that included the affixing of a memorial to the fallen of the Great War to an outside wall.

Situated directly on the A5 is the small village of Four Crosses, whose most prominent feature is its eponymous inn, which has served the needs of travellers for over 350 years. It was formerly a staging post for coaches taking travellers between London, Holyhead and Ireland. On one occasion the Irish satirist Dean Swift (1667-1745) stayed there, and vented his displeasure at the poor standard of accommodation afforded, and at the shrewish tongue of the landlord's wife, by scratching the following couplet on a window pane with his diamond ring:

> *'Thou fool! To hang Four Crosses at thy door!*
> *Hang up thy wife, there needs not any more.'*

Carved on one of the window lintels there is also the following monition:

> *'Fleres, si scires Unum tua Tempora Mensem;*
> *Rides, cum non sit forsitan una Dies.'*

which translates as:

> *'You'd weep and cry if sure to die before one month were past:*
> *and yet you play and sport away this one poor day,*
> *though it may prove your last.'*

The Four Crosses Inn was restored in 1926 and again in 2004.

Also included in Hatherton Parish is the village of Calf Heath, which has a very attractive non-conformist chapel. Here the Hatherton Branch of the Staffordshire & Worcestershire Canal formerly left the main line and passed northeast to Four Crosses, terminating at Catsbridge Lane. There was a toll collection point at Calf Heath.

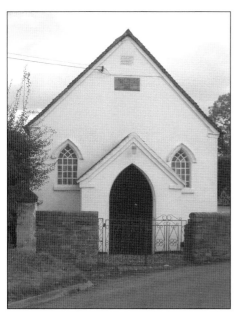

Left: **Calf Heath Methodist Church** stands on Straight Mile and was erected in 1860. A plain and simple design was lifted by the use of intricate and elegant cast-iron window, a pair of which can be seen here. Those used to light the main body of the church are larger and therefore even more delicate in their design.

Right: Looking northeast along the **Hatherton Branch** of the Staffordshire & Worcestershire Canal at Calf Heath. The branch continued east before ending at a wharf against Catsbridge Lane. There was formerly a toll collection point here at Calf Heath.

Left: **Hatherton Hall** was one of the district's first listed buildings, being so designated on 16 May 1953. Built in the Gothic style in 1817, it appears little altered externally, and is, reputedly, similarly so inside. Its setting, viewed across either parkland or water, is idyllic.

SAREDON

Formed from two hamlets, Little and Great Saredon, this parish lies south of the A5. The Saredon Brook, a tributary of the Penk, formerly known as that river's Cannock Heath branch, links the hamlets. This brook provided the energy for two powerful corn mills at Saredon and Deepmore, and was also renowned for the large number of trout it held. There was also a windmill in the middle of Little Saredon, which was built around 1640 and remained in use until at least 1872, its working life thereafter being slightly prolonged through the use of a portable steam engine to drive the stones. In 1942 the remains of the sails were removed and the tower was converted into a house for the proprietor of Hawkins Tile Works in Cannock. Little Saredon's other noteworthy feature was the disproportionately large number of yew trees that used to grow there. Great Saredon has a Roman tumulus on high ground, a quarter mile distant from, and facing, the A5.

Left: **High View Cottage,** Great Saredon, is a fine example of a timber framed cottage. It is unusually decorative in that the timber framing has diagonal braces and shaped studs. The massive central chimney stack is typical of houses with a 'baffle entry' floorplan and this house and the adjoining cottage are thought to date to the mid 16th century.

Right: **Mill House** and its windmill tower are a focal point in Little Saredon. This is a view south towards the mill, with Little Saredon Dairy and Farmhouse centre left. The latter is of early 18th century origin, the dairy part retaining its original low stone benches.

Above: The windmill site at **Little Saredon** was ideal; this was demonstrated by that fact that successive windmills were built there. Here, looking northwest, the last mill's prominence is evident. This tower mill replaced a wooden post mill dating from 1640.

Right: **Little Saredon Mill** must have done good business or else a portable steam engine would not have been brought in to power the stones when the deteriorated in 1872. In 1942 the remaining mill gear was removed and the present house conversion work undertaken. This is the mill tower in October 2004.

BREWOOD AND COVEN

Brewood

Brewood is one of Staffordshire's largest parishes. After the ice age a thawing glacier deposited sand where Brewood now stands and a 16 mile-long lake formed. When this dried up a forest grew in the alluvial mud, known afterwards as Brewood Forest. A Celtic earth fort, now called Beacon Hill, was built on a large mound in the forest; axe heads have been found here. The Romans conquered this earth fort and fortified it. After the Roman evacuation, for fear of the Picts and Scots, the Britons fled into the Forest, settled on the sandy knoll and burned down the Roman fort. They later claimed that its ruins were haunted, and called the woods between 'Breude' meaning 'fearful' or 'ghostly.' The knoll also took this name. In old Celtic is was pronounced Bre-oode, so when bishops came to hunt in the woods they wrote it down as Brewood, but it is still pronounced as Breude.

These Britons were probably Christians, and they built a church there. The Saxons certainly had one, as a stone coffin has been dug up in the churchyard, and lies near the south side of the Chancel. When the first Prebends of Lichfield were made in 822, the Dean became Prebendary of Brewood. The present church, dedicated to St Mary & St Chad, has 12th and 13th century origins, but has been repaired and restored a number of times, most notably between 1879-89, when these cost £6,124.

The Giffard family came to Chillington in 1178 and live there still. Giffard's Cross, near Brewood was erected to commemorate Sir John Giffard shooting a panther. The beast had escaped from the hall and was about to spring on a mother and baby when, Sir John's son said 'Prenez garde haleine, tirez fort,' – Take breath, pull hard, shoot well. Sir John did, and killed it from a long distance with his crossbow. A panther's head and this motto were added to his coat-of-arms. In Queen Elizabeth I's reign Peter Giffard was imprisoned in the Tower because he remained Roman Catholic. Afterwards he promised to reform and was released. The Queen visited Chillington and her bedroom remains, intact. The hall was badly damaged by Cromwell's soldiers in the Civil War; the estate was sequestrated but restored at the Restoration.

Brewood was so important in medieval times it became a corporate town, although it never had a mayor or a corporation. Older inhabitants were very cross if anyone referred to it as a village. Brewood flourished in medieval times, Kings and Bishops hunted there; forest Courts were held, and, after King John had disafforested the woods, King Henry gave the Bishops a Charter to hold a weekly market. Bishop Hurd, who refused to become Archbishop of Canterbury because he was too old, was one of the well-known and successful pupils of Brewood Grammar School. This was re-established by Dr. Knightley in Queen Mary's, after the endowments had been seized for Royal use.

In 1797 *The Gentleman's Magazine* described Brewood as: *'a small market town, situated on a gentle eminence seven miles from Wolverhampton. ...The situation of this town (or rather village) is rural, pleasant, and retired, and is a proper place of retreat from the bustle of large towns. ... In several hamlets in this parish considerable quantities of locks and other articles are made, but most of the inhabitants are employed in agriculture.'*

Hundreds from the Black Country, and other districts attended a fair or wake held every September to celebrate the Church's dedication. Bull baiting, cockfights, and stalls were among the amusements, and the wake was very noted and popular. Lock making became a staple industry. Then came the railway and because of prejudice, it had to make a detour to Four Ashes. Brewood became isolated, the workhouse went from Bargate to Cannock, the magistrates to Penkridge, lock makers to Willenhall, and for a time it was rather derelict.

Brewood is associated with a number of notable individuals, including:
Colonel Carless who was in the Royal Oak with King Charles, was born at Bromhall Brewood. He is buried in the churchyard. His gravestone was stolen in the early 20th century, but a small stone was erected, stating *'Near here lieth the remains of Colonel Carless whom the King did call Carlos, May 1689.'*

George Mason, grandson of Colonel Mason of Gunston Brewood, drew up the Virginia Declaration of Rights, upon which the USA's laws were based. His opening sentence, written on 26 May 1776, was *'That all Men are born equally free and independant, and have certain inherent natural Rights.'* This wording was incorporated into the opening of the Declaration of Independence, issued 6 weeks later on 4 July 1776: *'We hold these truths to be self-evident, that all men are created equal, that they are endowed by their Creator with certain unalienable Rights, that among these are Life, Liberty and the pursuit of Happiness.'*

Brewood was the birthplace of the civil engineering contractor Thomas Andrew Walker. He made the Severn railway tunnel (1879-86), underground railways in London, Buenos Aires docks, and Barry docks at Cardiff (1884-9). His greatest work was the Manchester Ship Canal (1887-94); completed after his death, at which time he was employing 24,000 people.

Coven

Coven is 2 miles southeast from Brewood. Its history predates the Norman Conquest, but the parish was only formed from the civil parish of Brewood on 2 July 1858. The church, dedicated to St Paul, dates from 1857 and was renovated in 1927. A chapel was also built in 1839. Near the village is the Park Farm, where, legend has it; a crock of gold was found. At the entrance to the Park Farm lane is Rock Bank, formerly known as Rat Bank, pronounced in Staffordshire parlance, Rot Hank, hence its present name.

Coven is an unlikely place for much industry, but there were once charcoal bloomeries for smelting iron. The burnt ruins of Forge Mill remained for many years. The village once had several lock makers, and the firm of Smith of Coven was a noted maker of machinery, whose loco engines were used in mines for many years. The first iron plough was also made at Coven.

During World War II, Coven was the site chosen for a dummy building & airfield site to attract enemy bombs away from the Boulton & Paul aircraft factory. This was both a day- and night-time decoy, and included mock Defiant fighters, the kind made by Boulton & Paul. With the changing pattern of air raids, use of the Coven decoy was discontinued in June 1942. Nonetheless, it remains a very rare and important site in the history of wartime defences.

Left: A view over Brewood from the vicinity of Tinker's Lane, with Dean Street on the extreme left and the spire of the Church of St Mary & St Chad prominent on the horizon.
Brewood Civic Society

Right: A close-up of the timber-framed cottages that formerly stood on the corner of Dean Street and **The Pavement**, Brewood. These were swept away for newer development in 1961.
Brewood Civic Society

Left: The people of Brewood always seemed to turn out for big occasions. This was scene in **Market Place** on the occasion of the funeral of Edward VII on 20 May 1910. The Boy Scouts precede the Fire Brigade, with civic dignitaries following. *Brewood Civic Society*

Left: **Market Place**, Brewood is neatly framed by impressive buildings, and made into a square by the staggered junction it makes with Stafford Street. Flanking the end of Market Place is the Lion Hotel, seen here in the late 19th century. *Brewood Civic Society*

Right: **The Lion Hotel** formed the backdrop to many photographs taken on great and small occasions in Brewood. The reason for this group being here is not know, but the fire pump forming the focus of the picture does look very new, so perhaps it was on the occasion of its entry into service. *Brewood Civic Society*

Left: A view down **Sandy Lane** in the early 20th century. This leads from Market Place to The Pavement, or on to Tinker's Lane, via Sparrow's End Lane. There seems little evidence of any form of transport other than horses or bicycles. For many years the shop on the left was the Post Office.
Brewood Civic Society

Left: One of Brewood's lost inns is **The Angel**, which stood on the corner of Bargate and Stafford streets. This is its frontage to the latter, which promised *'PURE HOME BREWED ALES.'* A small, planted, seating area occupies this site today. *Brewood Civic Society*

Right: **The Angel Inn** had an extensive yard with stabling, which can be seen here. It was not Brewood's main coaching inn – that was The Lion – but cater for the needs of its guests and customers', such as this gentleman and his young charge. *Brewood Civic Society*

Left: A procession makes its way from Bargate Street into **Market Place**, Brewood, c.1911. The occasion is not known, but flags are on display, so it could be Empire Day, or for the Coronation of George V. The banners for Powell's Tea Rooms in Bargate Street add to the festivities. *Brewood Civic Society*

DINNERS AND TEAS PROVIDED.

Left: Yet another Brewood Hostelry is **The Swan Hotel**, whose one-time proprietor – Arthur Marshall – went to the expense of having these postcards produced to promote his catering services. Marshall is listed as proprietor in a 1912 directory. The Swan is situated in Market Place.
Brewood Civic Society

Right: The procession on the previous page was marching past **Speedwell Castle**, seen again here from Stafford Street. William Rock, who died in 1753, reputedly built this imposing house from the proceeds of betting on the racehorse Speedwell. It is in the unusual architectural form known as 'Batty Langley style Gothick.' *Brewood Civic Society*

Left: **Stafford Street**, Brewood, contains a lot of timber-framed buildings, most of which were given brick façades in the 19th century. The view is towards Engleton Lane.
Brewood Civic Society

Left: James Gamson's hand-painted signs add considerable charm to this view of his 'Royal Bakery' premises. The smaller sign also promotes his other services: *'APPARTMENTS – TEAS PROVIDED – LOWEST TERMS.'* All of the family seem to have got into the picture, one way or another. *Brewood Civic Society*

Right: John Wakefield was running the Post Office in Market Place, Brewood in 1912. Kelly's Directory for that year records that in addition he was also a: *'baker, grocer, photographer, and wine and spirit merchant'* – he probably kept open late too! *Brewood Civic Society*

Left: Lawn Tennis became very popular at the turn of the 20th century, and the lawns of many large houses were given over to the sport each summer. Here a game between capped and uniformed schoolboys is in progress at the rear of the Grammar School.
Brewood Civic Society

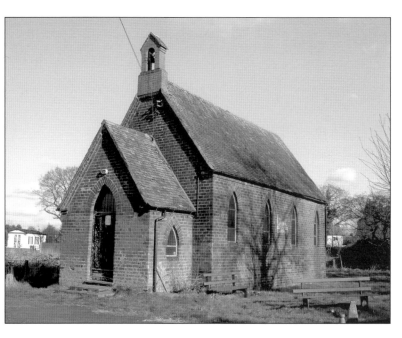

Left: **Coven Heath** was enclosed in 1850. This small chapel in Ball Lane was built there a few years later, but has now seen better days.

Right: **The Church of St Paul,** Coven, was completed in 1857 to designs by Edward Banks, architect, of Wolverhampton, who also remodelled a number of other churches in the district. He adopted a late-13th century style for the building. There had been a mission church in the village for a few years beforehand.

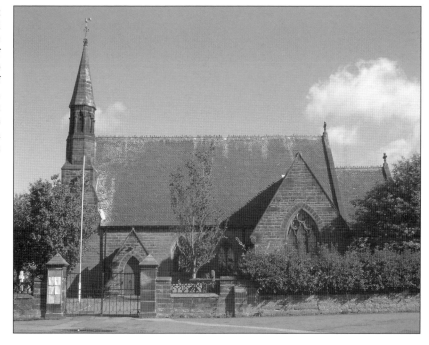

Right: This view down **Brewood Road** was taken in the 1930s, when popular motoring was in its infancy. Nonetheless, the landlord of the Anchor Inn has diversified and opened a tearoom at the side of his pub. *Wolverhampton Archives*

Left: Eight children stand and stare at the camera – was a parent behind it? They are standing on the towpath of the Staffordshire & Worcestershire Canal, close to Cross Green Bridge, Coven.

Right: **The Rainbow** was a noted Coven Inn for many years. The proprietor, William Baker, is seen here holding the horse whilst his family and staff stand proudly in front of the building to the right. *Wolverhampton Archives*

Right: **The National School** in Coven was held in the village Mission Church from 1854, and took over these buildings entirely from 1857, when the Church of St Paul was consecrated. These buildings have been added to over the years, but are a rare example of a mission church not being developed into full church. *Wolverhampton Archives*

Above: Another lost Coven Inn was **The Ball**. It stood on the Stafford Road at Coven Heath, by where the M54 crosses over. This view is from c.1910 when H E Holloway was proprietor. Its not hard to see why the place was a 'FAMOUS CALLING HOUSE', for the forecourt boasts at least three amusement machines, one of which is a test of strength, plus a weighing machine – hours of harmless fun! *Wolverhampton Archives*

CHESLYN HAY

Cheslyn Hay village and parish is situated 2 miles south of Cannock and 6 miles north of Walsall. Anciently it was part of Cannock Forest and belonged in turn to the Crown, to Sir John Dudley, who was executed by Queen Mary then to the Levesons, who passed it by marriage to the Lanes of Abbots Bromley. It was formerly extra-parochial and as such attracted many dissenters driven from the towns by the Clarendon code of penal acts. Many unsuccessful attempts were made to oust them and their settlement was of great concern to the Overseers of the Poor of Great Wyrley.

Nonconformity has always flourished here and in 1788 a Methodist Chapel was established, which was rebuilt in 1819. Salem was built in 1855 and rapidly established itself as the chief religious centre with a strong interest in music. The cast ironwork in front of Salem was erected in the same year, a Sunday school was added in 1889, the Chapel itself was enlarged in 1898 and a new organ installed in 1911 at a cost of £500. The employees at the Edge Tool Works of William Gilpin established another branch of the Methodists at Wedges Mills. David Buxton first brought Primitive Methodism into the village in 1810, a Chapel was erected in 1848, and Mount Zion in Cross Street in 1880.

The area was extensively mined for coal, iron ore and lead. Thomas Leveson had mines of coal and lead in 1636. Cheslyn Common was enclosed in 1797, and prior to this had been a extensive squatter settlement, whose inhabitants lived in mud huts. Cheslyn Hay village was formerly known as Wyrley Bank. It was transformed by the affluence that followed the growth of coal mining, which drove out most other trades, except that of ling-besom making. In 1834 there was one colliery from which the coal was taken away largely by the Wyrley & Essington Canal, opened in 1792. Edward Sayers had a coalmine at the Old Falls and the Coppice in 1851. Frederick Gilpin opened another in 1868. In 1872 Joseph Hawkins sank a mine near the Hatherton reservoir. The Nook and Wyrley Colliery closed in 1949 after being in operation for 75 years. In 1868 a brick and tile works was also opened in the parish.

The population grew from ten families in 1665 to 443 inhabitants in 1801, 2,560 in 1901, 3,232 in 1921, from which it declined to 3,130 in 1951. At one time some of the parents in the village were unmarried although they had lived together for years. This caused the village to be described in 1834 as 'almost as civilised as its neighbours.' The buildings of a growing community were added progressively from the late 18th century onwards: School (1839); National School (1875); Board School (1882); Fire Station (1908), Library (1924). Brick and tile manufacture was added to Cheslyn Hay's industries from the late 1860s onwards. Cheslyn Hay's coal industry began to contract from the 1880s onwards, but at a quickening pace immediately following the end of World War II. Dating from that conflict is the community centre, which was converted from a wartime decontamination centre around 1950.

Left: 100 years ago many of the district's parishes ran their own fire brigade. This is the complement mustered for Cheslyn Hay in 1908. The cart is a hand pump. In those days fire brigades were all voluntary, the only 'brass' to be had was the considerable amount that had to be kept immaculately polished on the helmets, uniforms and hose nozzles! *Salem Methodist Church, Cheslyn Hay*

Above: Sadly, many memorials to the fallen of the Great War were erected all around the country in the early 1920s. The one being unveiled here in Cheslyn Hay on 14 August 1921 was amongst the first anywhere. In 2004 the area around the war memorial is the subject of a landscape and village improvement design scheme to encourage villagers to focus on their identity and the history of the area. *Salem Methodist Church, Cheslyn Hay*

Left: Primitive Methodists established a chapel on Wyrley Bank in Cheslyn Hay in 1848. A **Mount Zion Chapel**, built in Cross Street, Cheslyn Hay, superseded this in 1880. This is seen in 1962, in a view looking from Low Street.
Salem Methodist Church, Cheslyn Hay

Above: In the days before sound films, running a cinema was not too technical a business, and many small villages had their own *'flicker palaces.'* Cheslyn Hay was no exception, and the Britannia Picture Co ran the Palace, which, if the somewhat hastily put up sign is to be believed, is doing good business, for everyone except dogs and ponies that is!
Salem Methodist Church, Cheslyn Hay

Above: Roman Catholicism was served in Cheslyn Hay by the opening of the Cheslyn Hay & Wyrley Mission Station in 1907. The following year its name was changed to St George's Mission Hall, outside of which the local Salvation Army are seen posing. The Catholics continued to use the hall until around 1912. *Salem Methodist Church, Cheslyn Hay*

Above: Multi-purpose general stores, like the one run by Geof Parkes in Cheslyn Hay in the 1950s, were the lifeblood of local communities. Looking at his list of provisions and services, there doesn't seem to be much he didn't offer!

SHARESHILL

Shareshill is situated 6 miles north from Wolverhampton and 3½ miles from Cannock. Vestiges of two encampments on the northeast side of the village are supposed, from their square form, to be Roman in origin. In the 12th and 13th century the area lay within the Royal Forest of Cannock. There was a mediaeval village at Shareshill, but most traces of this have been obscured. The oldest buildings in the present village are timber-framed cottages of 16th century origin. Its original church, dedicated to St Luke, dated from around 1558, but was barbarously destroyed in 1740, with only the tower, with its fine band of ancient ornament, surviving to be incorporated into its replacement, which was dedicated to St Mary. This was extensively repaired and beautified at the expense of Lord Hatherton in 1842, and a parsonage house was added in 1845. One of the former Vicars of the parish was the Rev. W. H. Havergal, father of Frances Ridley Havergal (1860-1876). The Church, more recently rededicated to both St Mary & St Luke, possesses a fine carillon of six bells.

Apart from the church, Shareshill has 3 other listed buildings: Woodberry House, Manor Farmhouse and a barn at Home Farm. By the Staffordshire Review Order 1934 part of the Parish of Saredon was added to Shareshill. A realignment of the main Cannock-Wolverhampton road in 1939 required the demolition of several buildings, including a pub, at the south end of the village.

Above: Another general store offering a wide range of services was that run by the Sawbridge brothers on the Cannock Road in Shareshill. Presumably, 'frozen foods' was put in inverted commas to flag up the novelty of stocking such items, or the store's innovativeness in stocking them – any other interpretation of this is otherwise a little worrying!

Above: The original caption to this postcard view reads: *'Shareshill Nr Post Office.'* It appears to have been taken in the first decade of the 20th century. A lone bicycle has been lent against the hedge, centre left, whilst in the distance a patient white horse waits harnessed to a two-wheeled cart. *Wolverhampton Archives*

Left: Dated 1908, this postcard depicts another general store adjoining the **Bull's Head** in Shareshill. The attention of the chap on the right seems to have been drawn to the man pushing the pram. Perhaps this was a rather *'liberated'* thing to do for the time. Also, the children in the pram seem old enough to walk. *Wolverhampton Archives*

Above: The Temperance Movement had its origins in Preston in 1832. With polluted water and chronic toothache rife, alcohol was both 'safe' to drink and a palliative to pain. Non-conformists had taken up the cause by the 1870s, and a National Temperance Federation was formed in 1884. Shareshill had its own **Temperance Hall**, which took the form of this 'tin tabernacle' in Elms Lane, which was erected in 1904 and late became the village hall. *Wolverhampton Archives*

Above: Shareshill's first school was opened in 1818, but a Parish School augmented this in 1841. A purpose-built school was erected in 1871, and this is seen here in a view looking from Saredon Road. The building was enlarged in 1914, roughly the date of this photograph. *Wolverhampton Archives*

Left: Shareshill's present post office and general store began life as a row of estate cottages. A legend over the door reads: *'A L V. 1894.'*, these being the initials of A L Vernon, Esq., of Hilton Hall. The pillar box, off camera to the right, bears George V's monogram, suggesting his reign as a likely date for the middle cottage to have assumed its present usage.

Right: A modern-day prospect of Shareshill taken from Little Saredon, with the tower of the Church of St. Mary & St. Luke very prominent on the horizon.

Above Left: There was a church at Shareshill by 1213, but this was appropriated to Penkridge College in or after 1225, and served as a Chapel of Ease to that Church. Shareshill was raised to parochial status in 1551, when it gained rights of burial. The oldest part of the present **Church of St. Mary & St. Luke** church is probably 14th century. The church of this date was rebuilt in c.1562, and the one seen today resulted from a second rebuilding c.1742. It is acknowledged as one of the finest Georgian churches in the Midlands. Originally the church was dedicated to St Luke, but later this was changed to St Mary the Virgin, and more recently the present compromise was reached!

Above Right: A close-up of the clock mechanism in the tower.

GREAT WYRLEY

Great Wyrley lies on the busy A34 highway between Walsall and Cannock. The Manor passed from the Crown to the de Loges family, to the Petos and, in the reign of the Elizabeth I, to Sir John Leveson. The Leveson-Gower family, later Dukes of Sutherland, held it until it was sold in 1914.

An ecclesiastical parish including Cheslyn Hay was established on 3 November 1846. The Church of St. Mark was built in 1845 in the Early English style on land given by the Bettson family. It has a chancel, aisles, nave, and a turret containing one bell. A lady chapel was added in 1945 to mark the centenary. The churchyard was cleared of most gravestones in 1952, and in 1956 a stone pulpit replaced the original wooden one. Nonconformity was established in 1787, but the first chapel was not built until 1846, and extended in 1857. A modern Wesleyan chapel was built at a cost of £2,500 on the Walsall Road in 1925. Streets Lane Primitive Methodist chapel was erected in 1906, another being established in a wooden hut in 1920 and replaced by a modern building on Walsall Road in 1927.

A National School was established in 1849 and continued until 1884, when Walsall Road Board School, later used as a primary school, replaced it. This was enlarged in 1906 and again in 1959. Another school was built at Landywood in 1907. This was used as a primary after the opening of a new secondary school, with its own playing field, in Station Road in 1939. A Working Men's Institute was established in 1871 and a library was built up. The Parish Council also maintained a library, but this was discontinued in 1949 when the County Council mobile service began. There were also three Working Men's Clubs: on the Walsall Road, at Upper Landywood and in Wharwell Lane.

The population grew rapidly after the Second World War. There were 75 households in 1665, 227 inhabitants in 1801, 800 in 1851, 1,687 in 1901, 2,701 in 1921, 4,287 in 1951, and over 5,000 today, Following the installation of a new sewerage system in 1957 building went on apace, with three extensive housing sites being added.

There are a few buildings of historic interest, of which the oldest is probably Landywood Farm; Fisher's Farm dates from the late 17th century; Wharwell Farm from the 18th century; Whitehouse Farmhouse was demolished in 1957, having been built by Thomas Corvesar in 1711. The Moat house, demolished in 1958, dated from the Restoration; nearby were the remains of a moat.

The chief industries of Great Wryley were coal mining and edge-tool manufacture. The Alports mined coal there in 1560 and Nicholas Parker used an early steam engine at his Wharwell Farm Colliery in 1750. William Gilpin sank a colliery in 1809, a further mine was established in 1860, and the Great Wryley Colliery opened a new plant in 1872. All these have been abandoned, the last mine to work being Harrison's No.3, which dated from 1896. The Edge Tool industry was brought to Churchbridge by William Gilpin in the first decade of the 19th century and was developed by his successors.

Above: This highly decorative street sign adorns a house in Great Wyrley. Its is white enamel on a blue background, and, with the recent loss of the old station building, the road name is about all that is left to remind local people that their village once had a railway station.

Left: Not that it was much of a station – sparse facilities to say the least were provided by these timber waiting cabins, which were typical of those provided by the London & North Western Railway in the 19th century. The line was built and opened by the South Staffordshire Railway on 1 February 1858. Passenger services were withdrawn on 18 January 1965, but coal traffic sustained the line long enough for these to be reinstated on 7 April 1989, but, sadly, no replacement station was provided at Great Wyrley.

Right and Below: The stationmaster's house in Great Wyrley was in Station Road, just where the line crosses over the road. It was an imposing two-storey building, which in later years was rendered over, obscuring the decorative refractory brick banding, revealed when the house was demolished to the level seen at right.

Left: There are few symbols of Great Wyrley's industrial past left. A striking example is the **Working Men's Institute**, situated on the Walsall Road at the corner of Norton Lane. Completed in 1871, this was built at a cost of £250 and could seat 250. It was used for concerts or lectures, and was supplied with newspapers and once had a small library.

Right: The foundation stone of the Great Wyrley Working Men's Institute was laid by Lt Col Harrison of Norton Hall on 18 July 1870. Money to fund the project had been raised by public subscription.

Left: Solidly built, using variegated brick, the Working Men's Institute is nicely detailed, including its name, finely carved above the main door. From 1964 onwards the local table tennis club used the institute.

Above: The **Church of St Mark,** Great Wyrley, was erected in 1845. It is built of stone in the Early English style. Electric lighting was installed in 1928 and a new reredos was added in 1939. Around 1950 the churchyard was cleared of all but two of its gravestones, one of which can be seen at right, as can the church's single bell on the roof.

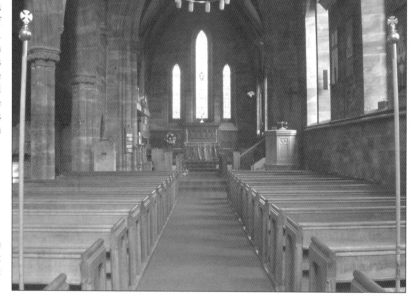

Right: The interior of the **Church of St Mark**, Great Wyrley. The stone pulpit seen at right was added in 1956.

HILTON

Hilton was amongst the lands donated to the Monastery at Wolverhampton upon its foundation in 994 by Lady Wulfrun. Hilton Manor House, as Hilton Hall was first known, was constructed by Sir John Swinnerton in the early 14th century. The Swinnertons lived there for two hundred years until Margaret Swinnerton married Henry Vernon in 1547. He was a descendant of Richard de Vernon, who had arrived from Normandy with William the Conqueror in 1066. The Hall, which was rebuilt in 1700, and extensively remodelled in 1830, remained in the Vernon family for 400 years, through 12 generations of Vernons. One such was Admiral Vernon who, in 1739, captured the Spanish stronghold of Porto Bello with only six ships and became famous for this throughout Europe. The Portobello Tower, which stands on the hill fronting the Hall, was erected in his honour. Admiral Vernon was nicknamed 'Old Grog' due to the boat cloak he wore habitually, which was made of a rough silk called grogram. In an attempt to stem drunkenness amongst his crews he forbade the serving of raw spirits and ordered that the two half-pint rations of rum or brandy served daily be watered down. This was very unpopular with the seamen of the day, who named the resulting drink 'Grog' in his 'honour.' Another member of the family who made his mark was Richard Vernon (1726-1800) a horse breeder, trainer and successful jockey. He was a founder member of the Jockey Club and known to his contemporaries as 'Father of the Turf.' Diomed, one of the horses he bred and trained at Hilton Hall, won the first ever Derby in 1780.

A curious custom was formerly practiced here. On 1 January each year the Lord of the Manor of Essington was formally bound to bring a goose to Hilton Hall, which he had to drive at least 3 times round the fire, itself being blown by 'Jack of Hilton.' This done, the goose was carried to the table, whereupon he would be handed a cooked meal. The Jack of Hilton in question was an œolipyle – a device for creating a blast by means of steam. Made from brass, this was shaped like a man kneeling on his right knee whilst covering his eyes with his right hand. Water was poured in at the back of his neck, heated by the fire, and escaped as steam through his mouth. This custom was discontinued when the two manors were owned by the Vernons.

Left: The various entrances to **Hilton Park** are guarded by gates. This set is on the far side of the property leading away to Portobello Tower. All of the gates had these decorative urns on top of the pillars, but this set is the only one that is complete, although the slenderness of their pedestals makes them look more precarious that they are in reality.

Above: **Hilton Hall** was home to the Vernon family for over 400 years. It has been extensively rebuilt at least twice, first in 1700 and later in 1830. When photographed here in April 1980, it was serving as a nursing home, and more recently it was the headquarters of Tarmac plc.

Above: A detail showing the central frontage pediment of **Hilton Hall**, with the coat of arms and motto of the Vernon Family prominently displayed.

Left: The architectural detail applied to **Hilton Hall** goes all the way round the house, as can be seen in this view of its rear, where decorative quoins and another form of armorial device can be seen.

Right: The chapel wing at **Hilton Hall** has yet another armorial device on its pediment and a version of the one seen above incorporated into the wrought iron gates protecting it. The candy-twist gateposts and foliage on the gates themselves are particularly well detailed.

Left: The **Portobello Tower**, which still stands on the hill fronting Hilton Hall, was erected in honour of Admiral Vernon, who, in 1739, captured the Spanish stronghold of Porto Bello with only six ships. Perhaps his most lasting legacy is use of the term 'grog' for the watered down rum ration he introduced in an attempt to reduce drunken behaviour on board ship. Admiral Vernon's nickname was 'Old Grog' after boat cloak made of a rough silk called grogram he habitually wore.

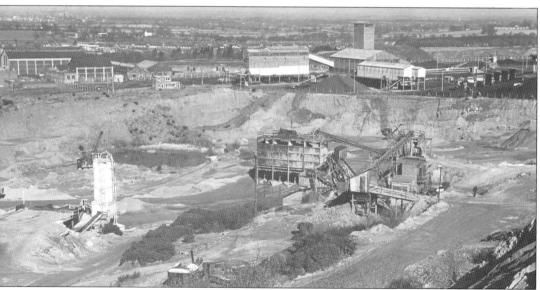

Above: Hilton's main industries were mainly extractive. In addition to its collieries – Hilton Main and Holly Bank – there has long been a large gravel pit off Bognop Road. By the time that it was photographed here it had gouged quite a large hole in the landscape.

FEATHERSTONE

The boundaries of Hatherton, Water Baton, Hilton, and Featherstone are described in the Charter of Wulfrun to the Monastery at Wolverhampton in 994. For centuries the parish belonged to the Deans of Windsor and Wolverhampton. In this charter, Brenesford, modern Brinsford, is mentioned. Sparsely populated, Featherstone's most celebrated resident was the antiquary John Huntbach.

There was little urban development in the area until the sinking of the Hilton Main Colliery, which brought in miners from widely separated coalfields. In 1921, the population was only 39, an increase of just 4 over 1851, but by the late 1950s it had risen to 1,500. To the original colliery estate has been added a larger number of council houses.

The only place of worship is a Methodist Chapel, which was erected in 1929. Under the Staffordshire Review Order, 1934, part of Bushbury was added to Featherstone.

A shopping centre has been created near to the Community Centre. The Centre was erected during the last war and today has a full-time warden. The Coal Industry Social Welfare Organisation has provided a Social Club, with extensive playing fields, on the Wolverhampton Road.

Left: **Moseley Old Hall** is of late 16th century origin, but was encased in brick c.1870. Henry Pitt purchased the estate in 1583; he was almost certainly the builder of Moseley Old Hall, for in 1600 the house was referred to as 'Mr Pitt's new Hall at Moseley.' His daughter Alice inherited the house on his death in 1602 and subsequently married Thomas Whitgreave. Alice and her son, also Thomas, gave sanctuary to King Charles II after his defeat at Worcester; he arrived from Boscobel House. This view shows part of the formal gardens.

Left: **Brookhouse Farm** stood close to Moseley Old Hall, but was also in the projected path of the M54. This photograph recorded the farmhouse as it was in March 1978.
Wolverhampton Archives

Above: In a 1940 directory, the **Red White & Blue Inn**, on the Cannock Road (A460) at Featherstone, had a 'New' prefix to its name, suggesting that there was an earlier pub of the same name. It is a fine example of a 1930s roadside inn, which still stands, but the generous car park in front has been taken into the widened road. *Wolverhampton Archives*

ESSINGTON

Essington for many centuries formed part of Bushbury parish, which until 1934 was part of Cannock Rural District but is now a populous suburb of Wolverhampton.

Coal, clay, and iron ore have been mined in Essington Wood since the Middle Ages. The coal has been mainly worked out or the mining of it is fraught with great difficulty. Brick and tile making is still carried on to a considerable extent. There are one or two small factories but the majority of residents work outside the parish. Most of the soil formerly belonged to the Vernons of Hilton who have disposed of a considerable amount of land in recent years. The Wyrley & Essington canal passes through the parish.

Essington was formed into an ecclesiastical parish in 1934 when the church of St. John the Evangelist was built as a memorial to the late J.W. Forrest of Holly Bank House. The former iron church with a tower containing one bell was originally served from St. Mary's, Bushbury, but was later a church schoolroom and a social centre. The vicarage was in the gift of trustees. There was an annual dole of £24 for the deserving poor of Essington, Bushbury and, Brewood. The Methodist Chapel was erected in 1883, is of red brick, and will seat 200 persons.

Housing development in the parish has been scattered. The parish covers 3,007 acres but there are several communities mainly based on the main roads that pass through the parish to Walsall, Wednesfield, Willenhall and Wolverhampton. There has been considerable suburban development since 1921, when the population was 2,393.

Right: Some of the clay mined in Essington was used to make tiles. This is part of the former G W Lewis Tileries Ltd site, photographed on 9 January 1980. The massive flue was to the kiln beyond, and the conveyor system was used to move clay around the site.

Left: The area around **Holy Bank** has been important to the history of Essington and Hilton. There was once a colliery of this name at the latter, and the Church of St John the Evangelist, Essington, was erected in 1933 in memory of the late J W Forrest of Holy Bank House. This is Holy Bank Farm, out towards Landywood, captured for a commercial postcard view. *Wolverhampton Archives*

Right and Below: Essington also once had a windmill, which stood just off **Bognop Road**. It was a post mill, the large timber superstructure being built around a central post: the whole being capable of turning to face the direction of the wind. Sheep were able to graze safely around it in 1904, but by April 1980, all but the main post, and some of the bearings upon which it rested, had gone. *Wolverhampton Archives*

BILBROOK

Bilbrook derives its name from the Moat Brook, which was formerly known as a brook in which 'billiers' (water plants such as watercress) grew. Recorded in Domesday, two main settlements developed, one, at Bilbrook itself, and another at Lane Green, to the south. Bilbrook's existence is closely related to that of Codsall, but until the 1640s these two separate settlements remained. At the latter date Bilbrook's development southwards extended into Codsall parish, and thereafter their history and development have been conjoined. Around 1805 Bilbrook House was built for John Egginton of Oxley, and this stood until the 1960s, when it was demolished to make way for housing. Holy Cross Mission Church was in Tettenhall Parish from until 1959, when it was transferred to Codsall Parish, becoming a district church in 1979. The building itself dates from 1898. Non-conformity also took root in Bilbrook, with John Wesley visiting there nine times in between 1751 and 1770. On his visit there in 1757 he was successful in forming a society of 20 people. Ten smallholdings were created in the southeast part of the area in 1921, and in the 1920s and 1930s many houses were built in the northeast part of Bilbrook, some of which were to house workers at the Boulton & Paul Aircraft Ltd factory, which opened in Pendeford in 1936. Further council and private house building after 1945 effectively merged Bilbrook, Lane Green and Codsall.

Above: **Bilbrook House** was built for John Egginton of Oxley around 1805. In the mid-19th century it was the home of the Wolverhampton iron merchant Joseph Tarrant, who may well be depicted in this early photograph. The house was demolished in the late 1960s to make way for a modern housing development. *Codsall & Bilbrook History Society*

Above: Bilbrook was expanded massively with the removal of the Boulton Paul Aricraft factory from Norfolk to nearby Pendeford in the mid-1930s as houses were provided for the workers employed there. One part of Bilbrook to be affected by this was **Lane Green**, which is seen here in its pre-expansion, rural days. *Codsall & Bilbrook History Society*

Above: There could be few better contrasts between the old and new Bilbrook's than that afforded by this view of **The Woodman** in the early 20th century, with the local hunt gathered on the green in front. Now the road has consumed the green. *Codsall & Bilbrook History Society*

Above: A further reminder of Bilbrook's rural origins comes from this photograph of **Holy Cross Church** in Bilbrook Road. This began as a mission church, and once had a small shop next to it, seen here, positively weighed down by enamel signs. Holy Cross came under Codsall Parish from 1959 and became a district church in 1979. *Codsall & Bilbrook History Society*

Right: As noted above, the cause of Bilbrook's massive expansion in the mid-1930s was the nearby relocation of the **Boulton Paul Aircraft factory**. During World War II this produced thousands of rotating gun turrets for fighter and bomber aircraft, and its own Defiant fighter aircraft – 1,062 of them – which were used as night fighters during the Battle of Britain and the Blitz. *Codsall & Bilbrook History Society*

Above: **The Greyhound Inn** formerly stood opposite The Woodman in Bilbrook. Photographed around the turn of the 20th century, at that time the landlord was Edwin Parker, who is probably the man in his shirtsleeves standing in the doorway. *Codsall & Bilbrook History Society*

Right: Another direction in which Bilbrook was formerly separated from urban development was in the direction of Wolverhampton. This is a view along Wolverhampton Road, **Birches Bridge**, c.1930. *Wolverhampton Archives*

CODSALL

Codsall is mentioned in Domesday as 'Codshale', with 6 persons recorded there and 8 in Oaken. Its early fame rested upon a sulphurous well located 'in a wood in the village' (north of Wood Hall Farm, by the Newport Road), which supposedly offered a cure for leprosy and 'scabs and itch in both man and beast.' This attracted visitors until the mid-19th c. The oldest part of Codsall is around St Nicholas Church, which has Norman origins, but the south doorway is all that remains from this. The rest was rebuilt between 1846-8 by Edward Banks, Wolverhampton's leading Architect of the period, who was also working on the Shrewsbury & Birmingham Railway, then building through the village. Banks chose the Decorative style for the church, and used locally sourced sandstone.

Codsall and Oaken developed quite slowly. In 1327 they had just 11 and 10 taxpayers respectively, and a Poll-tax assessment of 1641 recorded 105 people living in Codsall and only 53 in Oaken. By the late 18th c Codsall had begun to spread south along Church Road, and in the early 19th c it began to develop as a community. In 1818 a National School opened on the corner of Church Road and Church Lane, and included a lending library from 1833. The school moved to Chillington Drive in 1965. Codsall Wake was held in the first week of May, and included such delights and bull- and bear bating! Non-conformists worshiped in Codsall from the late 18th c. A Primitive Methodist Chapel was built in 1825, but proved unsuccessful. Wesleyans leased it from 1850, but it closed in 1876. Trinity Free Church, on the corner of Broadway and Chapel Lane, opened in 1874, partly replaced the chapel. The church moved to a new building on Histons Hill in 1967; the old one being demolished in 1968.

Codsall Parish became part of the Seisdon Poor Law Union in 1836, but the opening of the Shrewsbury & Birmingham Railway, with a station in Codsall, on 12 November 1849 changed its character irrevocably. Thereafter the village was a favoured residential place for Wolverhampton merchants and manufacturers. Development was rapid. A Post Office opened in 1851, followed by one at Oaken in 1864. From 1855, mains water was available from Wolverhampton, and supplied to Oaken from 1895. Pendrell Hall, a large residence to the northwest, was built in 1870. It was sold to Staffordshire County Council in 1955 and reopened in 1961 as a residential adult education college. By the 1880s Codsall had become a popular day trip resort. A refreshment room had opened by 1880, and by 1908 there were 3 of these, but only one remained by 1928.

In the late 19th c and early 20th c housing was built along Wood Road, and in the early 1920s the first council houses were built, in Station Road, followed by private houses and bungalows between Oaken Lanes and Histons Hill in the 1930s. A railway halt was opened at Billbrook in 1934, and an electricity supply was available from 1935. The pace of development did not slacken. In 1940 a Secondary School (now Codsall High School) opened in Elliots Lane; this was extended in the late 1950s in response to the building of a large council estate in the Wilkes Road area, and a leisure centre opened in its grounds in 1976. Codsall also grew in 1966 as part of Wergs was added from Wrottesley Parish. In the early 1970s, a bypass – Baker's Way – was constructed north of Codsall, and houses were built on its north side, and the remainder of the decade saw extensive house building.

Neither Codsall not Oaken ever became very industrialised. Agriculture had dominated from before Doomsday, and this was joined by market gardening from c.1850, reflecting the influence of the newly opened railway. Several sandstone quarries were opened on Histons Hill, Wolverhampton Road and Sandy Lane for the construction of the railway. They also served the church rebuilding, and the last of them worked until the late 1930s. There was a windmill north of the church. It is shown on Yates' Map of Staffordshire 1775. Thomas Nicholls was the miller there in 1834, and the mill worked until 1850. The brick tower survives, converted to a house.

Codsall was the birthplace of the sculptor Sir Charles Wheeler (1892-1974), and it was the adopted home of the artist Norman Thelwell (1923-2004), famous for his humorous illustrations of ponies and horses. Apart from the Church, Codsall has four listed buildings, and areas around this and the Square are designated Conservation Areas.

Above: **Codsall Station** on the Shrewsbury & Birmingham Railway, photographed in the 1880s, before the building of the footbridge. The buildings were the work of Edward Banks, one of Wolverhampton's leading architects in the 1840s-1860s, and reflected his favoured Italianate style. Then the station had seven staff; now it is unstaffed and the buildings have been converted into a pub. *Codsall & Bilbrook History Society*

Above: This view of **Station Road**, Codsall, is a near contemporary to that seen on the previous page. That most of the people have their backs to the camera would suggest that a train had not long called and the carriage at left is performing a u-turn. *Wolverhampton Archives*

Left: **The Pendrell Oak** was an ancient hollow tree which formed one of the parish boundary markers for Codsall Wood. It was something of great local celebrity, and was still standing in the 1950s. *Wolverhampton Archives*

Above: **Pendrell Hall** in Codsall Wood was built c.1870 for Edward Viles of Bilston, who was editor of the *Gentlewoman's Magazine*. In 1910 Frank Gaskell, who remodelled the house and built the lodge on the main road, acquired it. This view shows the Hall in 1913, after it's remodelling. *Codsall & Bilbrook History Society*

Above: The billiard room at **Pendrell Hall**, in which a remarkable level of natural lighting was achieved by the use of a large skylight. The Gaskell family sold Pendrell Hall in 1955, and in 1961 Staffordshire County Council opened it as a residential adult education college. *Codsall & Bilbrook History Society*

Above: Twenty people are seated in this charabanc, which is really just a rather stretched car. The post card is labelled 'The Court Cars' and may have been produced for promotional purposes. In the 1920s, when the photograph was taken, Codsall was a popular day-trip destination. Oddly, the driver is not seated on the very right of the vehicle. *Codsall & Bilbrook History Society*

Above: An old tradition in parishes was the annual ceremony of *'beating the bounds'*, when parishioners toured the boundary points and markers. Originally this had a serious purpose, that of ensuring that the boundary was secure and had not been breached. By 10 June 1935, when this party was photographed prior to departure, it had become more of a ceremonial activity, and this was the first time the bounds had been beaten in 25 years. *Codsall & Bilbrook History Society*

Above: **Codsall Wake** was traditionally held in the first week of May each year. In the early 19th century it offered both bull and bear-bating, but by 1927 the event had become the May Fair, and here is that year's May Queen and her attendants. The gentleman standing to the right is Frank Gaskell of Pendrell Hall. *Codsall & Bilbrook History Society*

Above: **Oaken Lane** flooded on a number of occasions in the early 20th century. Six people are in, on and astride this early motorcar, which was presumably stranded in the floods, or else the lad in the sailor suit would have been a tad uncomfortable sitting on the engine! *Codsall & Bilbrook History Society*

Right: **St Nicholas Church,** Codsall, depicted in 1797. There has been a church on this site since the 12th c. The building seen here was the work of many hands over at least four centuries. All but the tower was rebuilt to the designs of Edward Banks, the leading Wolverhampton Architect, between 1846-8, using local sandstone. *Codsall & Bilbrook History Society*

Left: Just before he commenced his work rebuilding **St Nicholas Church**, Edward Banks made a series of pen washed drawings of it, one of which is seen here. This is a view from the northwest.
Codsall & Bilbrook History Society

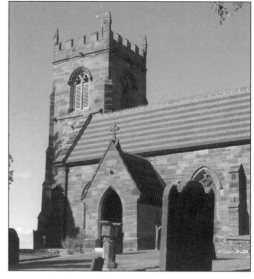

Right: Edwards Banks' completed church of 1848. He chose the Decorative style for the church and used sandstone quarried locally in Histon's Hill. The tower housed a clock and 8 bells, but these were recast and re-hung in 1936, and 2 new bells added. A new organ was installed in 1927, when the church was redecorated.

Left: **Codsall windmill** stands to the north of the church, and was erected around 1775. It was still working in 1851, but its tower was converted into part of a house in the latter part of the 19th century.

Right: There were several sandstone quarries on or around **Histon's Hill**. These were opened up to provide materials for both the Shrewsbury & Birmingham Railway and the rebuilding of St Nicholas Church. One quarry, on the south side of Wolverhampton Road, was worked between the 1880s and late 1930s, before being infilled. It is seen here just before the site was developed for the offices of South Staffordshire Council.

Above: **'Codsall Chapel'** was in fact Trinity Free Church, which brought together all of the non-conformist religions present in the village. Built at the junction of Broadway and Chapel Lane in 1874, it served this purpose until a replacement opened on Histons Hill in 1967. Sadly, the old Trinity Church was demolished the following year.

Above: **Codsall Wood** was first inhabited in the 14th century, but remained sparsely populated until the 20th century. Arrayed along a road leading to the A5, it eventually had three pubs to tempt passing travellers, and also a Tea Pavilion, by the gate to which the lady in white is standing. *Wolverhampton Archives*

Above: A second view of the area around **Codsall Station**, sometime early in the 20th century. The station drive is to the right, but quite why these seven girls are standing the way they are is a mystery. *Codsall & Bilbrook History Society*

Right: **Oaken** is in the southern part of Codsall Parish. Its name is of Old English derivation, but the area was not populated significantly until the 17th century. After the coming of the Shrewsbury & Birmingham Railway in 1849, numbers of large houses were built, especially on Oaken Lanes, as residences for Wolverhampton industrialists. This view is of Shop Lane in the 1920s. *Codsall & Bilbrook History Society*

Above: At the start of the 20th c **The Crown Hotel** was run by the Malpas family, some of whom may well be standing proudly outside. Salt & Co's Burton Ales & Stout was served. Comparing this view with the one above highlights the considerable number pf changes that were made to the pub in the first half of that century.

Above: This postcard showing **Codsall Square** was posted in 1912. At that time J Reynolds ran The Central Stores. The area was still very much dependant upon horse-drawn vehicles, as the state of the roadway attests.

Above: By the late 1940s **The Crown** was an Atkinsons house and had been remodelled to include two prominent bay windows on the ground floor. An area in front of the pub had also been set aside to provide car parking.

Above: By 1949 the **Central Stores** were being run by B & J Housden, but had otherwise changed little. The electric streetlamp outside The Bull Inn is very impressive.

Left: There were many small businesses in Codsall. One such was this tiny grocer and fruiterer's shop in **Chapel Lane**. The sign on the window notes that a new shop is opening on Monday October 19th, which may have replaced this one. The little bridge crosses a stream, which is now culverted.
Codsall & Bilbrook History Society

Right: Dairies were important to the local economy, and there was one at **Oaken Manor Farm**, seen here in the late 1940s. The business was run by W M Iliff, and they delivered only Grade 'A' Milk according to the side of their van. *Codsall & Bilbrook History Society*

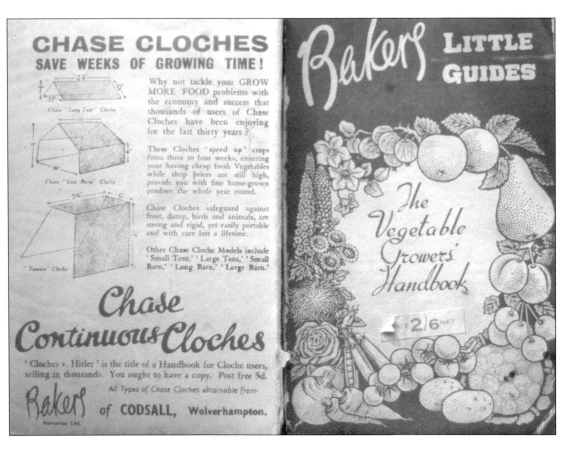

Above: There were nurseries and market gardens in Codsall from the 1850s onwards. Perhaps the most celebrated was Bakers, who had relocated to Codsall Hall Farm from Wolverhampton around 1904. Here they thrived, and their 'Little Guides' and other catalogues, served to make the name of Codsall more widely known around the country. The business closed in the late 1960s, but the name is perpetuated in that of Bakers Way, the Codsall by-pass, which passed through their site. *Codsall & Bilbrook History Society*

Left: Codsall now has a large Co-op Superstore, but its antecedent was this branch of the Wolverhampton & District Co-operative Society in Church Road.
Codsall & Bilbrook History Society

PATTINGHAM AND PATSULL

Pattingham

Pattingham is a small but expanding village 6 miles west of Wolverhampton and 4½ miles southwest of Codsall. It lies about halfway between the ancient British camp at Wrottesley and the Roman camp at Chesterton, and originally served as one of the estate villages to nearby Patshull Hall. There are more than 4,000 acres within the parish boundaries, over 1,500 being in the little township of Rudge. The land is mainly arable.

The most notable building is the ancient church of St Chad, part of which dates from the 11th century. Its priest is mentioned in Domesday Book, but there was a Saxon church here long before that. Sir Gilbert Scott, the eminent architect, and his sons, restored the church, with the generous help of the Earls of Dartmouth, its Patrons, during the latter half of the 19th century. The lichgate is a fine decorative timber framed feature, and in the churchyard are a sundial and an old stone cross. Inside the church, the reredos, stained-glass windows, and peel of eight bells are amongst its other treasures.

The Dartmouth Estate cottages are very distinctive and form the core buildings of interest in Pattingham Conservation Area.

Patsull

Patshull abuts Shropshire and is 3 miles southwest from Albrighton and 9 miles west from Wolverhampton. The area is dominated by Patshull Park, in whose grounds the church is situated. Patshull Hall, formerly the home of the Earls of Dartmouth, was built from c.1750 to designs by Gibbs, and is currently undergoing restoration. It is believed to be the largest listed building in Staffordshire. During the Second World War most of Patshull Hall was lent to the Royal Hospital for surgical cases; it also housed soldiers and sailors. After the war it was also used as a rehabilitation centre for crippled men.

In the grounds stands the Church of St Mary, which was erected in 1743, is in the Italian style. It will seat 200 people and was thoroughly restored in 1874. All around the house and the church lies Patshull Pool, which covers an area of 85 acres. Altogether the hills, the rocks, tile woods, and the water combine to make a lovely scene. For many years the Patshull Estate was owned by the Astley family, who disposed of it to Lord George Pigot, one of Lord Clive's generals. After holding it for about a century the Pigot family sold it to Lord Dartmouth.

Half a mile west of Patshull House lies Burnhill Green. There, at the end of Beckbury Road, stand two notable buildings, one of which used to be a coaching inn and is now a private residence. On the opposite corner stands the Memorial Hall, built in 1904 in memory of his father and mother by the sixth Earl of Dartmouth. It was used by the Women's Institute, and also for entertainments and dances, for children's dinners, and for all village meetings. In 2003 it was converted into a private house.

Above: A late 19th or early 20th century postcard view along **Wolverhampton Road** at Newgate in Pattingham. *Wolverhampton Archives*

Above: This view along **High Street** in Pattingham is a near contemporary of the one above. Only human or animal powered transport is on evidence. It is possible that the tricycle belonged to the photographer. *Pattingham Local History Society*

Above: A series of approaches to the centre of Pattingham, all taken in 1949. The first is along **Westbeech Road**, where the schools are visible centre right. There had been some form of education provided in the village since 1596, but these buildings were erected in 1875 following a bequest made by the late Benjamin Matthews, which had become effective on his widow's death the previous year.

Above: The west end of **High Street** in 1949.

Above: Looking along **High Street** into Wolverhampton Road. The timber-framed cottage, left of centre, is the same one as can be seen in the photograph on the top of page 89.

Above: A view along **Clive Road** looking away from the centre of Pattingham, with a lone cyclist on the wrong side of the road.

Left: A village celebration with the participants pausing to be recorded for posterity in between the lichgate to the Church of St Chad and the Pigot Arms in High Street, Pattingham, in the first decade of the 20th century. *Wolverhampton Archives*

Above: These rather smartly dressed workmen are taking a breather during the course of erecting a new timber **Village Hall** for Pattingham in October 1922. Lord Dartmouth gave the site for this to the village, which was opposite the east end of the church.

Above: The form of the hall can be seen more clearly from further away. Timber buildings of this kind, many of which were war surplus, were very popular just after the Great War.

Above: This **Village Hall**, seen to here to the left of the church, served Pattingham well for 44 years, being replaced by a more permanent structure, which was opened in February 1966.

Above: **Patshull Hall** is arguably South Staffordshire's finest country house. It was built c1750 by James Gibbs (1682-1754) to replace an earlier hall. It was then extended in 18th century and again in mid- to late-19th century, and altered. This view is looking back up the main terracing at the rear of the hall. *Wolverhampton Archives*

Right: Inside the kitchens at **Patshull Hall** at 14.46 one afternoon in the early 20th century. Tall spacious kitchens like this were the norm for large country houses. Those on display at Shugborough Hall are very similar to these. The seat of the Earls of Dartmouth, Patshull Hall passed to the Crown in 1958 in lieu of death duties. After many years of neglect, it is currently being sensitively and lovingly restored.
Wolverhampton Archives

Right: This triumphal entry and flanking screen walls protect the inner courtyard at Patshull Hall. Like the house, they are the work of James Gibbs and date from c.1750

Left: **The Church of St. Mary** was also built to designs by James Gibbs, and was consecrated in 1743. It was enlarged in 1874 by the pushing out of the north side, this work being paid for by the 5th Earl of Dartmouth. The Church is now vested in the Churches Conservation Trust and on the occasions when it is open, it is well worth a visit.

PERTON

Perton was formerly part of the parish of Wrottesley, which stretched from Kingswood in the south to Pendeford in the north. Until the mid-1930s it was almost entirely agricultural, containing about three hundred houses. The Lord of the Manor, Baron Wrottesley, resided at Wrottesley Hall, a beautiful mansion standing in a picturesque park. In 1897 Wrottesley Hall was burnt to the ground and the present Lord Wrottesley, a bachelor, built a smaller residence, where he now lives with his brother.

During the Second World War part of the park was taken over by the Dutch Government for a military training camp and part for an airfield. The Dutch camp was then taken over by Seisdon Rural District Council for conversion into housing.

It was not until the arrival of three great factories, the Goodyear Tyre & Rubber Co. (Great Britain), Ltd., Courtaulds, Ltd., and Boulton Paul Aircraft, Ltd., that the northern side of the parish, formerly known as Wrottesley Detached, developed. Perton is divided into two watersheds, the Trent and the Severn, which produces the phenomenon that surface water feeding the outgoing streams finds its way to the Rivers Trent and Severn respectively, with a final outlet, one into the North Sea, and the other into the Bristol Channel.

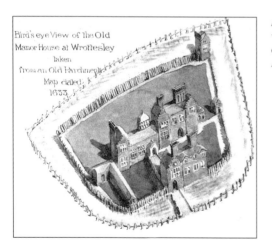

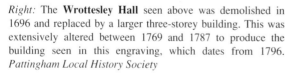

Left: **Wrottesley** had a moated manor house in the middle ages, which, by 1633 had been developed to this extent. Despite the changes made, the moat remained intact.
Pattingham Local History Society

Right: The **Wrottesley Hall** seen above was demolished in 1696 and replaced by a larger three-storey building. This was extensively altered between 1769 and 1787 to produce the building seen in this engraving, which dates from 1796.
Pattingham Local History Society

Above: The rear of **Wrottesley Hall**, before the great fire there in 1897. A smaller replacement hall was built on the foundations of this one in 1923, a scheme that managed to incorporate much material salvaged from the fire.
Codsall & Bilbrook History Society

Left: Another lost house from Perton was **Perton Grove.** This stood close to the boundary with Wolverhampton in Perton Road. It was built in 1855 for the Wolverhampton solicitor Henry Underhill, and stood for almost 90 years, being demolished in 1964.
Wolverhampton Archives

Left: **Perton Hall** stood southeast of the junction of the Pattingham road and Jenny Walkers Lane. Its origins were 14th century or earlier, but by the 1630s it was in a ruinous state. Repairs were made in the 1680s, but by 1820, when sketched here, only one gable end remained.
Pattingham Local History Society

Right: A second sketch view of **Perton Hall** from 1820. *Pattingham Local History Society*

Left: In 1941 a hutted camp was constructed along the southeast edge of Wrottesley Park to house Dutch troops. Here one of the main camp buildings is nearing completion. The Dutch occupied the buildings until 1947.
Pattingham Local History Society

Right: The Dutch Camp was not the first military use to which land at Perton had been put. In 1916 and 1917 an aircraft landing ground was used there, which, in 1941, former the basis of an RAF airfield. This had a very short operational life, being closed late in 1945 and the site being given back for agricultural use in 1947. Some buildings survive however, including this officer's quarter block.

Left: Another substantial survival from **RAF Perton**. This tall shed was used to train bomb-aimers, who would be held in cradles suspended from the roof, and look down upon a rolling map of the parts of Germany they were to attack, such as Dusseldorf.

LOWER PENN

The parish of Lower Penn is a pleasant country district extending from the Bridgnorth Road to the edge of Penn Common, round the southwestern boundary of Wolverhampton. Although it retains its separate identity as a civil parish, it is, for ecclesiastical purposes, included in the large and ancient parish of St. Bartholomew, Upper Penn, whose 13th century church looks out over the common to the spire of Wombourne. According to Prebendary Hartill's History of Penn this division of interest between Upper and Lower Penn goes back through the centuries to Norman times, and he records that for about 300 years after the Norman Conquest the name of Nether Penn was temporarily forgotten, the district being known as Penn Buffar after the owners of the estate, who in the 14th century became lords of Nether Penn, Orton, and Wombourne. It is interesting that the old feudal association between these places has its modern counterpart under the regis of the Rural District Council.

Along the ridge known as Springhill some of the finest views in the Midlands may be obtained, from the Malverns in the south, past the Clee Hills to the Wrekin in the west, whilst northwards the horizon is bounded by the heights of Cannock Chase. Along this ridge, also, may be seen some lovely examples of modern country house architecture, in happy contrast to the perfect Elizabethan setting further down the hill, where the black and white thatched cottage known as Walnut Tree Kennels, with its gay flower borders, nestles at the corner of Market Lane.

Many of the houses in Lower Penn have long associations with the past, but perhaps the most interesting is Trescott Grange, whose connections go back to the days of King Ethelred and Lady Wulfruna. Again quoting from Prebendary Hartill, we find that in the Middle Ages it was the country home of the monks of Combe, in Warwickshire, the outlines of whose fishponds can still be seen. The old dovecote is an interesting feature of this house, and there is a tradition that King Charles II was hidden here on his way to Boscobel. A few minutes' walk across the fields brings one to Furnace Grange, another large and progressive farmstead. It is almost certain that this was originally the Grange Furnace of Trescott, and we know that there were several furnaces or forges situated along the Smestow Brook used for iron smelting; the brook provided the waterpower for driving the bellows and the vast forests the fuel for the furnaces. Penn was then a clearing in the forest and the staple industry was sheep rearing, as evidenced by the number of small streets or alleys in the Wolverhampton area still bearing the name of 'Fold.'

A more modern touch is found at Dimmingsdale, where one of the large pumping stations built by the former Wolverhampton Waterworks is situated. Seen at night, with its brilliant lights reflected in the pool close by, it appears as a strange invader of this essentially country district, and it is much to be hoped that Lower Penn will retain its rural character in the years to come.

Above: The **Penn Common Brewery** was built by John Millard of Netherby Hall, Gospel End. On site there was a good supply of spring water and nearby were fields of malting barley and cereal crops. The brewery also had its own malthouse. The Penn Brewery Co Ltd was registered in October 1887 and was itself taken over in 1897 by the Burton Brewery Co Ltd. who sold it on to the Wolverhampton District Brewery Ltd in August 1899, who closed it down soon afterwards. Following closure the building was purchased by James Lakin, a local farmer, who took down the chimney, removed the pitched roof, and gave the building its present ornamental look.

Above: Simply entitled *'On Penn Common'*, on the horizon is the silhouette of the Penn Common Brewery in its original form, complete with chimney. *Wolverhampton Archives*

Above: Penn Common also had some pubs, one of which was the **Barley Mow**, which sold Frank Myatt's Ales. *Wolverhampton Archives*

Above: **The Greyhound**, on the corner of Greyhound Lane and Market Lane, is one of the centres of life in Lower Penn, as it the Victory Hall, which is hidden by the pub in this view taken in 1979.

Above: Part of Lower Penn's charm comes from the narrowness of its lanes and their hilly nature, both qualities which combine to good effect to produce views like this one.

Above: For many years the **Church of St Anne** was vital to the life of Lower Penn. The church is seen here left of centre in a view of Spring Hill Lane from the mid-1950s.

TRYSULL AND SEISDON

The parish of Trysull and Seisdon consists of two country villages, situated 6 miles southwest from Wolverhampton, 8 miles north from Stourbridge, and 7½ miles northwest from Dudley.

Trysull

The Church of All Saints' stands in the centre of Trysull. It is a 12th century building and inside there is an old chest constructed out of a tree trunk, surrounded by iron bands. This chest was used as a bank for church moneys. In 1725 John Rudge bequeathed the sum of £1 per year for the purpose of engaging someone to send dogs out of the church and for rousing sleeping people!

An old monastery existed at one time in Trysull, but this has now been converted into a private dwelling house and is known as Woodford Grange. Another noteworthy building in the village of Trysull is Trysull Manor, which was built in 1633. It is a pleasant old house and bears the following inscription over the front door:-

'Stranger should this catch your eye,
Do a favour passing by,
Bless this house ere you be gone,
And it shall bless you passing on.'

The old cobbled yard, coach house, and stables of this manor bear witness to an age when modern methods of communication were unknown.

The character of the village was changed and enhanced by following the acquisition of Trysull Manor by the Mander family in the late 19th century. They turned this 17th century timber-framed building into an exemplar of the Arts & Crafts Movement, and spread this style around the village through works they endowed, such as the village institute the late Howard Mander had built there in 1896. The village school is also nicely detailed.

Old corn mills in both Trysull and Seisdon were operated by waterpower provided by a stream known as the River Smestow. For a while after the use of waterpower was discontinued electricity was used. Trysull also had an old forge, which remained in use for many years and was at one time the home of Turner Sports Cars Ltd.

About a quarter of a mile from the centre of Trysull is a hill known as Fiershill, which is said to have been used as a site for the ancient beacons, which were lighted to warn the villagers of hostilities.

Seisdon

The village of Seisdon appears to have some historic connection with the ancient Seisdon Hundred Roll, which is the Domesday division of the county supposed to be named through its originally containing one hundred families of freemen. Its history is largely indivisible from that of Trysull, but it did become the base for the Seisdon Poor Law Union, which formally came into being on 17 October 1836. An elected Board of Guardians, 19 in number, representing its 12 constituent parishes, oversaw this. A new Seisdon Union workhouse was erected in 1858-60 at Trysull. It was designed by George Bidlake & Lovatt of Wolverhampton, and could accommodate 120 inmates. Some of the buildings survive but are derelict and inaccessible. The main building was demolished in 1963 following vandalism. Its main legacy is the name of Union Lane, just outside Trysull.

Above: Approaching Trysull along Trysull Holloway, looking towards the **Church of All Saints**. Cyclists and horses clearly abound. The cottages to the left have an almshouse style, but also show clear influence of the Arts & Crafts Movement, favoured by the Mander family. *Wolverhampton Archives*

Left: The thatched cottage on the right stands on the corner of **Trysull Holloway** and has had a colourful life. In recent years it was turned into a country club called The Thatches, but more recently has been turned back into a home once more. *Wolverhampton Archives*

Above: **Seisdon Hall** is one of two large houses in the village, the other being Seisdon Manor. The Hall has 17th century origins but the main fabric dates from the 1840s.

The Church of All Saints, Trysull, is of 12th century origin, but with many additions and changes. It was enlarged, in the Norman style, in 1844, and again in 1889, when it was also reseated, and an organ installed. The register goes back to 1561. The living was annexed to that of Wombourne until 1888. Below is a view taken inside the church during the works of 1889. *Below: Mrs Granger Above: Wolverhampton Archives*

Above: Both Trysull and Seisdon had water corn mills. **Trysull Mill**, seen at top, was built in its final form in 1854. It had a bakery associated with it, housed in the buildings centre right in the top right-hand photograph. The mill at Seisdon is shown in the bottom picture. It is both smaller and older, being dated 1749. Like Trysull Mill, that at Seisdon has been converted to a house. *Wolverhampton Archives*

Left: **Trysull House** stands on the corner of Seisdon Road and Trysull Holloway. Its brick façade masks the fact that it has timber-framed portions to the side and rear. This view is from the 1930s, when they were offering potatoes for sale.
Wolverhampton Archives

Above: This remarkably sharp postcard from the 1950s shows some of the more picturesque buildings from the two villages.
Wolverhampton Archives

WOMBOURNE

The village is situated on the main Wolverhampton-Stourbridge road, about 4½ miles south of Wolverhampton. It has existed from Saxon times, and is mentioned in the Domesday Book of 1086. The name is derived from Old English Womburnan, which means 'the winding stream.' The old hamlets of Blakeley, Orton, and Houndsdale (now corrupted to Ounsdale) which have all been established from the same early times, are now practically part of the main village.

Apart from two old farmhouses at Orton the church and the Wodehouse are the only buildings of interest. The oldest parts of the church are the 14th century tower and the spire, which dates from a hundred years later. With the exception of the north aisle, the rest of the church is modern. In the 12th century the church belonged to the Cluniac priory at Dudley, which also acquired by gift about this time a vergate of land in Wodeford, and monks living at what is now Woodford Grange served the church at Trysull.

In Wombourne church, near the main door, is an alabaster tablet carved to depict the parable of the Good Samaritan. Sir Samuel Hellier brought it from Italy in 1720. The church possesses valuable plate including an early Elizabethan chalice and paten (1560-1570), and a very fine silver repousse dish having a ship in full sail, of early sixteenth century Portuguese workmanship. The registers date from 1570 and there is a list of incumbents from the year 1180.

The Wombourne Wodehouse is situated about a ½ mile from the church and originally dates from the 13th century, though the present building in its attractive grounds is Jacobean with some earlier work. It contains a wealth of oak carving and four-poster beds, and an Elizabethan figure called the Silent and Good Woman.

Wombourne centre provides an archetypal view of the English village with its core of historic buildings looking out onto a village green, with cricket pitch and tennis courts. The South Staffordshire Railway Walk is very popular. Based around a former GWR line which only served the village for 7 years, between 1925 and 1932, this skirts through the rural edge of the Black Country and links with Wolverhampton's Valley Park. South Staffordshire Council's Leisure Services Department has published a series of Leisure Trails covering Awbridge & Trysull, Baggeridge Country Park, Orton, Wombourne, plus the railway itself, all of which radiate from Wombourne and the Railway Walk.

The Staffordshire & Worcestershire Canal winds its way through Wombourne, where can be seen one of the most famous landmarks on Britain's inland waterways –Bratch Locks – the country's first three lock staircase, and a significant feat of engineering ingenuity by James Brindley, and highly efficient in its use of water. Bratch Locks look out upon Bratch Pumping Station, a fine Gothic building of 1896 which houses a pair of steam-driven pumps.

Left: Patients and staff at the **Seisdon Rural District Isolation Hospital** in Clapgate Lane, Wombourne. All of the patients appear to be children, and five little faces peer down from the upstairs windows, determined not to be left out of the picture.

Mrs Granger/Wolverhampton Archives

Right: The Staffordshire & Worcestershire Canal winds through Wombourne, and is seen here at **Giggety Lane**, as a horse works a boat past another one, which seems to be listing over rather precariously.

Left: Constructed by James Brindley, **Bratch Locks** are one of the major engineering triumphs of the canal. Originally built as a three-lock staircase, the flight takes the canal through a vertical interval of 30 feet. Fragments of the original work can still be seen but the staircase was converted at an early stage into three conventional locks separated by 'pounds.' Two very large side ponds accept the excess diverted water produced from the upper two locks, and in 1927, when much reconstruction took place, a large weir was built.

Left: Facing Bratch Locks stands a handsome water pumping engine house in red brick with polychromatic brick and Venetian Gothic architectural detailing. The Bilston UDC Waterworks Company originally built this in 1895 at a cost of £6,300. It houses a pair of triple-expansion vertical steam engines by Thornewill & Warham of Burton-on-Trent, named 'Victoria' and 'Alexandra', each of which is capable of raising 1 million gallons of water in 20 hours from the boreholes 150 feet below where they stand.

Right: **Bratch Pumping Station** when new, before it was obscured by tree growth. The steam engines were decommissioned in 1960 but remained in situ, Victoria being restored to full working order between 1991 and 1996 by local steam engine specialist Len Crane.

Left: **Bratch Pumping Station** is opened to the public several times a year, when Victoria is steamed and operational. This view shows the main gates from Bratch Lane.

Bratch Station, Wombourne.

Above: Just up from the pumping station is the former **Wombourne railway station**, alongside the South Staffordshire Railway Walk. This is the track bed of the former Great Western Railway Stourbridge-Wolverhampton line, which was begun in 1913 but only completed in 1925. This view shows the station when new.

Left: Between May 1925 and October 1932 a passenger service was operated along this line. Today it is a leisure walk and the Wombourne Station building has been turned into a café and information point for this. Sadly, this waiting pavilion was demolished.

Above: A view across Wombourne from the line of the present A449 around the start of the 20th century. The bridge takes the road over the Wom Brook. To the right is the rear of the Red Lion Inn, whilst a team of four horses draws a wagon towards the bridge. *Wolverhampton Archives*

Above: A closer view across a growing Wombourne. The spire of St Benedict Biscop pierces the tree cover to the rear, and back of the Methodist Chapel in Mill Lane, with its prominent oriole window, stands proud of the surrounding buildings.

Left: **Red Lion Hill** in the 1930s. Before the construction of the A449 dual carriageway, this was the main road between Stourbridge and Wolverhampton. Little space was wasted on the inn sign. Its post informed patrons that the pub had a car park, and that it stayed open until 10.30pm. The post also served as a Midland Red bus stop.

Right: Butlers had many houses in the area, and several in Wombourne. The Red Lion was there's, as was **The Vine Inn**, High Street. The large vehicle to the right is a Sentinel steam wagon, which was made in Shrewsbury. These made ideal dray lorries and were favoured by breweries to distribute their beer.

Left: Looking along **High Street.** The two large waggons laden with hay standing near to Millbrook House are reminiscent of the importance of Wombourne as a farming village.

Left: **Church Road**, Wombourne. The single-storey building to the left has since been cleared to form an access road, whilst the house, left, is now a greengrocer's which does a thriving trade. The wall to the right once surrounded the green.

Right: Wombourne has one of the largest village greens anywhere; so large in fact that it can accommodate a cricket pitch. Here a match is in full swing. So quintessentially English is this view that it has been used by *The Times* no less to illustrate various articles.

Left: **Nailers Row** in Giggety Lane, Wombourne. Nailmaking was one of a number of Black Country 'cottage' industries, which, although centred upon The Lye, could be found in many places during the 19th and early 20th centuries. One such was Wombourne, where, nailshops could be seen behind cottages in a few places, but none more concentrated than here. The cottages survive, but in a modernised form.

Above: This view of **Botterham Lock** and The Boat Inn on the Staffordshire & Worcestershire Canal was taken in the first decade of the 20th century. It is rich in detail. At least some of the smartly dressed party on the towpath must have come there by bicycle, whilst the men in the background are some or all of the crew of the boat that has just worked down the lock. *Wolverhampton Archives*

Right: Whilst Wombourne retains many old buildings and much small village charm, in some areas it has changed beyond recognition. One such is **Windmill Bank**, the top of which once looked like this. The cottages are very typical of hundreds once seen in South Staffordshire.
Wolverhampton Archives

HIMLEY

Himley is a small village and parish on the main Stourbridge-Wolverhampton road, 1½ miles northwest from Kingswinford and 4 miles west from Dudley. There are no shops, post office, or school. The area of the parish is 1,185 acres. The Church, dedicated to St. Michael & All Angels, built in 1764, is a small brick and plaster building, well lighted by large windows characteristic of the period.

The name Himley appears in various forms. In Domesday Book it is spelt Himilie, and elsewhere as *Himelilega and Himlele*. All versions mean a clearing in a wood where hymele is grown. There is some uncertainty as to what hymele is, but it is either the hop plant or something like it.

Two buildings are of historical interest: Himley Hall and Holbeach House. The former, says Mr. Pitt in his *Topographical Dictionary*, 1817 is the seat of Lord Viscount Dudley & Ward, Lord of the Manors of Sedgley, Himley, Swindon, Kingswinford, and Rowley Regis. In 1946 the Hall was sold and after spending some years as the headquarters of the National Coal Board (Midland Division), it is now owned by Dudley MBC, who use it for events and exhibitions.

Holbeach House was involved in the Gunpowder Plot of 1604. Several of the conspirators fled from Stourbridge to Holbeach, pursued by the Sheriff of Worcester *'With the power and force of the country.'* The fugitives were only forced to appear after fire had been set to part of the house, and from the fact that Catesby was killed outright and three others were fatally wounded, we may assume that they resisted fiercely. Afterwards the Sheriff reported that *'the rest of that rebellious assembly is dispersed.'* Guy Fawkes never appeared at Holbeach, since he was imprisoned in the Tower of London immediately on his capture on the night of 5th November.

Little remains to-day of the blade mills which, according to an 1831 Topographical Dictionary, made Himley locally famous for *'a peculiar sharpness to edge tools.'*

The Crooked House pub, on the way to Gornal Wood, is just within the boundary of the parish of Himley. Formerly known as The Glynne Arms, it takes its name from the all too evident effect that mining subsidence has had upon it.

Left: **Himley Hall** was built in the 18th century by demolishing a medieval manor house on the site. Capability Brown designed the grounds, and William Atkinson enlarged the hall between 1824-7. The home of the Earls of Dudley, the hall received regular royal patronage: Edward VIII spending the weekend before his abdication there. During World War II it was used as a Red Cross Hospital, and sold to the National Coal Board in 1947, being bought by Dudley and Wolverhampton councils in 1967. Dudley MBC took it over fully in 1988.

Left: The corner of School and Stourbridge roads, Himley, in 1947. At one time all of the houses in Himley village were associated in one way or another with the Hall. To the right, off camera, leads Cherry Tree Lane, along which is an 18th century icehouse. These large, part buried brick domed structures were popular in the 18th and 19th centuries. Storing ice allowed large houses to offer the popular delicacy of ice cream to their guests.

Above: Sometime in the early 20th century a meet of the local hunt has brought Himley to a halt. The focus seems to be **The Dudley Arms**, which began life as a house in the late 18th century. Amongst the cyclists in the right foreground is the local policeman, but it is doubtful that his services were required. The houses seen above can also be seen centre right.

Left: In our cover picture, someone has a good vantage point from which to survey **Baggeridge Colliery** – the last of the working Black Country pits – possibly at or just after its closure in 1968.

Right: The first boreholes at Baggeridge were drilled in November 1896, but the project did not start well: the boring rods broke and leaving £200 worth of diamonds in the ground! Further borings revealed a coal seam at 600 feet. The first shaft was built in February 1899 and in July 1902 a seam of coal 24 feet thick was discovered. *Wolverhampton Archives*

Above: A second shaft found the same seam of coal in 1910, but the sinkers had to fight a sea of water for 19 months, finally keeping this out by the use of cast-iron segment plates fixed for 40 yards in the shaft. Baggeridge Colliery came into full production in 1912. This picture, and the one above, shows the surface buildings soon after this date.

Below: In the early 20th century **Baggeridge** afforded a striking contrast between the developing colliery and the woods surrounding it. The latter, seen here, were a popular destination for day-trippers.

Above: **Baggeridge Colliery** began making bricks in 1936 using locally occurring Etruria Marl clay and colliery shale, the bricks proved to be in such great demand that in 1944 Baggeridge Brick was created as a separate company. Here workers erect a stack at the brickworks. The colliery itself closed on 1 March 1968. It used pit ponies right up to its closure, one if which is seen here.

Left: Gospel End links Penn Common with **Baggeridge Wood**, which has been a local beauty spot for centuries. On 27 May 1825, Elisha Whitehouse wrote in his journal that: *'We all went with Dr. Waterhouse and Prudence Caddick to Baggeridge Wood – Lord Dudley's park and gardens. Drank tea at the Keeper's – rained nearly all the way back to Sedgley. Supped at Waterhouse's.'*

Above: A genteel picnic at **Baggeridge Wood** around 1900. For some curious reason a further two young ladies have been scratched out of the image to the right of the group left of centre, plus a man to the right of central tree! Some boys on the right are perhaps locals, intent upon their own pursuits.

Above: A view along **Gospel End Road** looking towards Wombourne in the early 20th century. Two ladies stand outside the Post Office, possibly waiting for a bus. The older of the two is dressed in austere black, whilst the younger one is in her Sunday best and carrying an umbrella – perhaps rain was expected then too!

Left: The **Mission Church of St Barnabas** in Gospel End, was built in 1846 during the Anglican expansion of the period. It is seen here c.1900, but has now been converted to a private residence.

SWINDON

Swindon, Swineduna, Suidon, and Sevindon all mean Pighill, and it does seem that the connection with Kingswinford means that Swindon was in a pig-rearing area for some centuries before and after Domesday. More recently Swindon, formerly on the edge of Kinver Forest, and having a plentiful supply of charcoal, was connected with the iron trade. In 1696 one George Foley was assessed for a levy for repairing the churchyard wall at Wombourne in respect of 'Swin Forge.' Dud Dudley is also thought to have made use of this forge for his early ironwork experiments. Later the ironworks were in the hands of Alfred Baldwin & Son, and subsequently Richard Thomas & Baldwin rolled, annealed, tinned, and finished steel sheets there.

There is an earthwork near Greensforge, which is probably a Roman fortified camp. The Kingswinford-Greensforge road passes through the middle of the camp, which measures 206 yards by 160 yards. Apparently it used to be known, for reasons unknown, as 'Wolverhampton churchyard.'

The church, dedicated to St. John the Evangelist, was built in 1854 of local sandstone and in the Gothic style, as a mission church under Wombourne. It was not until 1 January 1867 that it became a separate parish. The civil parish of Swindon was formed out of Wombourne on 1 April 1896.

The Smestow Brook formerly provided power for several large corn mills in the village; remnants of two of these are at Mill Farm, Smestow and Greensforge Farm, whilst another at Hinksford was demolished some years ago. An old disused malthouse remains in the centre of the village, and at one time there were in existence several nail shops where nails were made by hand and taken weekly to Kingswinford for sale. On the parish boundary with Kinver at Hinksford the former Seisdon RDC developed a large caravan site.

Left: A view down **High Street**, Swindon, early in the 20th century. Only the dog seems blaze about the camera. On the left is the junction with Hinksford Lane, at which stands The Old Bush Inn. The stones surrounding the tree outlasted what they were designed to protect, and sometimes perplexed locals and visitors alike. *Wolverhampton Archives*

Left: The same tree can be seen in this contemporary view looking up **High Street**, Swindon. The end cottage on the corner of Wombourne Road was then the Post Office. The sun dazzles the children in the centre, whilst those on the right are playing with a box cart. *E J Williams/Wolverhampton Archives*

Above: **The Church of St John the Baptist**, Swindon, was built in 1854 to designs of William Bourne. It is built from pink sandstone and stands on a hill north of the village. An organ was added in 1872 and the lichgate was dedicated in 1885.

Right: Snapshots that were taken to record family members or cars often recorded much more besides. This view taken in **The Holloway**, Swindon, in the 1930s, is looking towards High Street. *E J Williams/Wolverhampton Archives*

E P & W Baldwin ran an enlarged Swindon Forge from 1866. This specialised in the production of sheet iron. In these two photographs from 1913, engineers from Galloways Ltd, of Hyde Road in Manchester, unload and install new rolling mill machinery at Baldwins. Galloways specialised in manufacturing this kind of equipment.
Wolverhampton Archives

Swindon Forge began as a water corn mill, which was converted into a forge by Thomas Foley after he leased it in 1647. It passed to the Homfray and then the Thorneycroft families, before being leased to the Baldwins, who eventually bought it in 1899. The photograph top left is of the works at that date and shows the investment that the Baldwins had put into it, notably during the 1870s. In 1945 the works became Richard Thomas & Baldwin Ltd and specialised in rolling silicon steel sheets for the electrical engineering industry. Top right, a mobile crane by Morris of Loughborough is unloading iron from a canal barge. Below, a study in concentration as a team of workers feed sheet into a pair of rolls. Closed in 1976, and demolished, the site of the works is today marked by the names of Swinforge and Baldwin ways for the roads of housing that replaced it. All 3 images courtesy of *A W Robinson/Swindon Collection*

BOBBINGTON

Bobbington is a small village and parish on the Shropshire border, 8 miles northwest from Stourbridge and 6 miles west-by-north from Kingswinford. The settlement there is long-standing, and was formerly based around the church, which has 12th century origins. It is wedged against the Shropshire border by the Parishes of Seisdon, Trysull, and Swindon to the northeast, and Enville and Alvely to the south. It is one of the smaller parishes, covering some 2,681 acres. The ancient parish boundaries can in places still be traced by the remaining meerstones marking the Claverley-Bobbington boundary and the granite boundary stones on Blacklands.

Bobbington is still wholly agricultural as when Bobba the Saxon founded it, and Lord Helgot held it at the Domesday survey. An early Helgot built the two water corn mills and the small Norman Church of St. Mary, which has a 13th century font. In the porch is a 12th century stone effigy of the founder; a great yew, equally as ancient, stands in the churchyard. Originally in the Royal Peculiar of Brug (Bridgnorth), later in the Hereford diocese, the church is now attached to Lichfield.

Outstanding names in the history of Bobbington include Rickthorns (13th to 17th century), Dickens (15th to 18th century), Brook (15th to 19th century), Pratt (15th to 19th century), and the Corbets, first of Whittimere then of Blakelands. The free Church of England School of White Cross was founded in 1798 by Ann and Mary Corbett, daughters of Edward Corbett, a Justice of the Peace in the 18th century. This school was later rebuilt but subsequently demolished by the Air Ministry and replaced by a prefabricated building.

The Victorian Squires Moseley, of Leaton Hall, the largest landowners of the 19th century, helped considerably in improvements to the church, school, and village life, supporting the Severn Valley Farmers' Club, which met in Bobbington once every five years. They organised the enclosure of the common land in 1827, carried by Act of Parliament.

The Royal Oak Inn, the Red Lion, and Six Ashes Inn, all serve the scattered population and visitors.

Bobbington's only cottage industry, namely that of nailmaking, finished in the 19th century. At that time the area was noted for sport, with both donkey and greyhound races being held there. Bobbington has 10 listed buildings, including Leaton and Bobbington halls, plus 3 other fine houses. The hamlet of Halfpenny Green, 1 mile northeast of Bobbington, has a vineyard that produces and sells wine, and also has a Working Craft Centre. Flying lessons can be taken at Wolverhampton Business Airport, which is based on the former World War II airfield at Halfpenny Green, which opened in 1941. Blakelands Country House Guest House and Restaurant offers locally sourced food, accommodation and facilities for functions and weddings.

Left: Bobbington's existence predates Domesday, and even in the late 1950s it remained the epitome of the rural idyll: with narrow, gated roads, and stockmen droving cattle to and from milking.

Right: **Six Ashes** was named after the six ash trees which stood there until 1793, from when their numbers began to be diminished. This late 19th century view shows the eponymous inn there (left), at a time when the main Stourbridge-Bridgnorth road ran closer to the buildings than the line of the present A458. In the mid-19th century, although predominately rural, Six Ashes also had two nail makers.

Left: The Air Ministry built an airfield at Bobbington in 1941. Works to expand this in 1944 required the demolition of a farm and nailer's cottages at Gospel Ash, and the village school. Sold on for civilian flying in 1963, the airfield became a centre for flying lessons and small business aircraft, as this late 1960s advert shows. Monthly Sunday, and Bank Holiday, markets have also been held at the airfield since 1974, but recent proposals for a massive expansion of the facilities, at what is now called Wolverhampton Business Airport, mean that this advert's opening words have become very prophetic.

ENVILLE

The parish of Enville lies on the Stourbridge-Bridgnorth road, about 5½ miles from Stourbridge and 8½ miles southeast of Bridgnorth. The earliest recorded name of the village was *Efnefeld*, and under that name it is entered in Domesday Book. The three ancient manors of *Enfield, Lutely, and Morf* comprise the present parish. In the twentieth year of William the Conquerer, Enville (to use the name by which it is now known) was held by a Saxon, Alric, one of the King's Thanes, but the great overlord of this district was William FitzAnsculph. In the course of time William de Birmingham became possessed of the manor, and two of his descendants were Rectors of Enville, namely Roger de Birmingham (1273-1307), and Sir Fulk de Birmingham (about 1347-1370).

In 1422 John Lowe, of Whittington, was lord of Enville, and was succeeded by his son, Humphrey Lowe, Sheriff of the County of Stafford, in 1441. The only daughter and heir of the latter, Eleanor, married Robert Grey, third son of Reginald, Lord Grey of Ruthin, and it is recorded that their son Humphrey, in 1484, was the owner of the Manors which form the present parish of Enville. Since that date the family of Grey has owned Enville. Enville Hall, which once boasted its own private racecourse, remains a private house, but it hosts occasional events each year. Nearby Four Ashes Hall is available for weddings, receptions, corporate events and country pursuits.

The church has a Norman nave (about AD 1100) and a Transitional chancel (built by Roger de Birmingham, AD 1272-1307) and despite extensive restorations in 1749 and 1871 the distinguishing features remain. The present ornate tower is a copy of a style often seen in Somerset, and was built in 1871, when the original tower was taken down. Evidence of an earlier church on the site is to be found in a small stone figure of Saxon origin built into the arcading above the south aisle. Local tradition identifies this carving as a memorial to Saint Chad, the first Bishop of Lichfield. It was probably the porch niche figure of the original church.

Above one of the Norman columns of the nave is a stone carving of eastern origin, probably brought to Enville by crusaders. There are three crusaders' tombs in the churchyard, facing the west window. In the chancel are four beautifully carved miserere stalls. In the south aisle is an alabaster tomb of fine workmanship, dated 1559, to the memory of *'Thomas Grey of Enveld esquier and Anne his wyfe ...'* Within the altar rails on the north side of the chancel is the mural tomb of Roger de Birmingham, Rector of the parish from 1273 to 1307, and who rebuilt the chancel. In the churchyard stands an ancient cross with broken shaft, and nearby is a yew tree of unusually fine shape and size.

Left: For many centuries **Enville Hall** has been the seat of the Earls of Stamford. By the mid-16th century Thomas Grey had replaced the mediaeval manor house there with a brick house, which was greatly altered and extended over the years. Much of what had been done was lost on 25 November 1904 when the hall was ravaged by fire. First tackled by the Hall's own brigade, the intensity of the blaze drew in reinforcements from nearby towns. Here, the Stourbridge *'steamer'* is engaged in damping down. Only the west end of the house escaped serious damage.

Right: From 1848 onwards the gardens at **Enville Hall** were enlarged to designs of John Pope & Sons, nurserymen, of Smethwick. Centrepiece of this work was this massive Gothic and Moorish conservatory, designed by Grey & Ormson of London. Erected in 1855, the conservatory was used for just over 70 years, being partially dismantled in 1928; the rest being demolished in 1938 – a very sad loss.

Left: Another part of the **Enville Hall** redesign was the installation of fountains in the pools northeast of the house. A 4 million gallon reservoir was built to feed these, the water being fed to these by a pair of steam engines. One of the fountains could throw up a jet over 180ft!

Above: A view of **Enville** village from the edge of the Churchyard. Between 1816 and 1877 the main Bridgnorth Road (now the A458), running left-to-right across the image, was a turnpike road. The impetus to turnpike the road came from Bridgnorth farmers needing better access to Stourbridge markets. Each month the turnpike trustees met at The Cat Inn at Enville, which was deemed to be midway along the road.

Above: The first recorded reference to **The Cat Inn** at Enville is in 1777, and by the 1830s it was a calling point for thrice-weekly coach and omnibus services to Bridgnorth, Kinver, Stourbridge and Wolverhampton. Here it is the meeting point for the local hunt. Until 24 October 2004 the Cat did not have a Sunday licence.

Above: Between 1816 and 1877 **The Cat Inn** at Enville was also the meeting place of the Trustees of the Stourbridge-Bridgnorth Turnpike, it being more-or-less exactly midway between both towns.

Above: **Four Ashes Hall** was first built in the late 16th century, and by the late 17th century was the home of Henry Wollaston. Through marriage the estate and hall passed to the Amphlett family, the last of whom was still in residence there in the early 1980s. The house was rebuilt in the 18th and 19th centuries to form the hall seen here. Part of the earlier development included a stable courtyard and farm building complex.

KINVER

Kinver is very rich in Royal and ancient history, and its name is derived from 'Chene Vare,' meaning 'A Royal Rose.' The village lies at the foot of a straggling range of hills. These hills were much used in ancient times as observation points and strong posts for the defence of the locality. The Romans used the hills for that purpose and there are still traces of a large Roman Camp on Kinver Edge, 300 yards long and 180 yards wide. Wulphere, the first Christian King of Mercia, fortified Kinver Edge during the 7th century and there are still traces of these early defensive earthworks.

From the 7th century until the Norman Conquest the earl who ruled Mercia owned the land. After the Norman Conquest the Norman kings made it a 'Royal Manor and Forest.' The forests were much used by King John during his reign who, when hunting in the locality, took up residence at Stourton Castle, which is still in excellent condition, and occupied. At Stourton Castle are recorded many incidents of murders, Royal births, sieges, and the Civil War.

At the extreme eastern end of the cliff top stands the magnificent old church of St Peter's of the Rock dedicated to the memory of the first King of Mercia's two murdered sons, Wulphad and Ruffinus. In the church are monuments with the arms of the families of Hampton Grey, Worwood, and Compton (Comber) of Kinfayre Hall. A document, in which Charles I confirmed to the tenants and inhabitants of Kinver the privileges granted by previous Charters, is preserved in the vestry of Kinver Church.

The district is very rich in traces and evidence of ancient Troglodyte dwellings. These dwellings were cut out in the sand- stone rock and can still be found at Gibraltar, Dunsley; Holy Austin Rock; Nanny's Rock; and Meg-o-Fox Hole. Some of the rock houses have been restored and are opened by The National Trust.

At one time, Kinver was busy with several splitting mills and forges on the banks of the River Stour. These works have all been closed and no longer exist.

Kinver Edge, with its many acres of gorse, woodland, and heather, is now also owned by the National Trust, and this delightful spot, with its lovely views of the grand surrounding country, makes an ideal tourist resort. The area has a long and illustrious history as a focus for tourists. Kinver's long High Street, with a variety of building styles and periods, is centred on mediaeval burgage plots which stretch back to the River Stour on one side, and Church Hill on the other. The village is well provided with shops for locals and tourists alike, and a wealth of places to eat and drink.

Many thousands of visitors come every year to Kinver, which has for long been known as the Switzerland of the Midlands. This name was given to it by the British Electric Tramways Company, whose Kinver Light Railway brought tens of thousands of people there annually from all parts of the Black Country. The line operated from 5 April 1901 until 8 February 1930, and would have proven to be the most enormous tourist magnet had it survived.

Left: In stark contrast to the jollity which usually accompanied most of the journeys made on the **Kinver Light Railway**; this was possibly the most sombre use to which it was put in its 29 years' existence. The Rev E G Hexall had founded the Bethany Boys Home in Kinver, and when he died in January 1915 his funeral cortege comprised a pair of trams, with a small truck coupled between them on which rested his coffin. Seen here on the roadside between The Stewponey and Ridge Top Wollaston, this unusual assemblage made a unique journey by tramway all the way to Spon Lane Cemetery in Oldbury.
History of Wollaston Group

Right: A milk cart from **High Park Farm**, which is situated between The Stewponey and Wollaston. Milk deliveries like this, direct to customers from dairy farms, were the norm 100 years ago. The milk would be served straight from a churn into the customer's own jug. To serve the farms along its route, in late 1901 the Kinver Light Railway began a daily run collecting milk churns and vegetable produce, returning empties later in the day.
History of Wollaston Group

Left: During the first quarter of the 20th century, the lower part of **Bridgnorth Road**, as it descends towards The Stewponey, was developed for housing. A wide variety of architectural styles were chosen for these houses, a number of which were bungalows, such as Beech Lawn in Stourton, seen here. The popularity of bungalows was heavily influenced by knowledge of, or direct contact with, India. Those who built them had often spent some time in the Raj, and sought to retain something of this in their choice of housing.
History of Wollaston Group

Left: One bungalow that found other uses is the one situated opposite the site of The Stewponey at Stourton. This has been a café for the better part of 100 years, and remains in this use today. Stopping off here for an ice cream or a cup of tea has long been a welcome respite, especially for those walking or hiking the 5 or so miles between the Black Country conurbation and Kinver.
History of Wollaston Group

Right: For almost 200 years the junction between Bridgnorth Road and Prestwood Road at Stourton was dominated by a public house with an intriguing name: The Stewponey. Seen here in 1903, with **Kinver Light Railway** toastrack car No.50 passing, the building had stood since the early 18th century and was properly named the Green Man. The origins of its more distinctive and unusual name are obscure. Four 'theories' abound. It is: a corruption of Stouri pons – Latin for 'bridge over the Stour'; named after an inn called The Pony and a nearby pond or 'stew'; named after 'stepony' a kind of ale or raisin wine; or a corruption of 'Estepona', where a former tenant was barracked during the reign of Queen Anne..
History of Wollaston Group

Left: By the 19th century The Stewponey was in fact two adjoining inns. The second, seen here at right, was called The Foley Arms, and the correct name for joint hostelry was **The Stewponey & Foley Arms Hotel.** In this view the chap at left is leaning against a traction pole for the Kinver Light Railway. This is the same pole seen to the left of the pub above, and the one that remains today, behind the Kinver Parish Council notice board. The Stewponey catered for many horses, and one of the bell pushes seen on the porch reads 'Ostler.'
History of Wollaston Group

Left: The **traction pole,** referred to on page 136, is all that remains to give a clue as to the relative location of the old Stewponey inn, although this photograph, showing its demolition late in 1935, also helps. In the mid 1930s the main A449 at the Stewponey was widened to create a dual carriageway section and to eliminate a horrendous junction at which the Kidderminster and Wolverhampton roads met slightly apart and were linked by a short length of road which required two 90° turns to negotiate. Seizing the opportunity for increased patronage thus afforded, the brewery owning The Stewponey replaced it with a modern motoring hotel.

History of Wollaston Group

Right: The new Stewponey boasted accommodation, bars, restaurants, a ballroom, and, most of all a **lido** – a large open air swimming pool, which was immensely popular during the summer season. Changing tastes and times saw an inevitable decline in the lido's use, and its maintenance became less and less of a priority to its owners. The pool was demolished in the 1990s, a few years ahead of the pub itself. Lidos are now a scarce building type in the UK, and the loss of the one at The Stewponey, which was an exemplar of the form, is very much to be regretted.

History of Wollaston Group

Left: **Prestwood Hall** was the seat of the Foley family, who acquired the manor of Kinver in 1672. Sir John Lyttleton had built the original house, but this was replaced in the 19th century by a mansion in the Gothic style, seen here. Only the gateway from the original house remained The Foley family sold Prestwood Hall in October 1917.

History of Wollaston Group

Left: Whittington became a sub-manor of Kinver around 1200. Dating from the latter half of the 16th century, The **Whittington Inn** was a private house until 1788, when Lord Stamford ordered that it be turned into an inn, to replace one in Horse Bridge Lane, which became Bathpool Cottages, and is now known as Whittington Old House. Extended to the north in the 18th century, its location on the main A449 has always ensured that 'The Whitt' enjoys good patronage.

Right: **Stourton Castle** began as a Royal hunting lodge in the late 11th century, when William II, the son of The Conqueror, was known to favour the area. The lodge was enlarged to become a castle in 1195-6, but this was entirely built from timber. More permanent structures gradually replaced the timber ones from the late mediaeval period onwards. This engraving shows Stourton Castle in 1820, when it was the home of Elizabeth Grazebrook.
History of Wollaston Group

PHOTOGRAPH TAKEN ON THE OCCASION OF
2000 WORKMEN IN THE EMPLOY OF W. O. FOSTER, ESQ., M.P.,
MEETING AT STOURTON CASTLE, APRIL 23RD, 1867,
TO PRESENT AN ADDRESS TO WILLIAM HENRY FOSTER, ESQ.,
ON HIS COMING OF AGE.

G. H. Tora, Photo.   STOURBRIDGE.

Left: The Stourbridge ironmaster James Foster leased **Stourton Castle** in 1832 and paid for extensive alterations and additions to the buildings, all to the designs of Sir Robert Smirke. Following his death in 1853, James's nephew, William Orme Foster, lived at Stourton Castle. This card commemorated the coming of age of William Henry Foster on 23 April 1867, when 2000 workmen in his father's employ presented him with an illuminated address. The following year, W O Foster moved out of the Castle to Apley Hall near Bridgnorth.
History of Wollaston Group

Left: Between The Stewponey and Kinver the light railway ran along its own privately reserved track, which was fenced along its entire length and gated at each end. One of these gates can be seen here as toastrack car No.51 waits while a lady boards before its sets off cross-country to Kinver.
History of Wollaston Group

Right: The Kinver Light Railway's route between The Stewponey and Kinver was a compromise. P H Foley, the single landowner concerned, objected to the tramway company's preferred route, and to appease him it was agreed to thread the line along the sliver of land that separated the River Stour and the Staffordshire & Worcestershire Canal. This protected Mr Foley's farmland, but made the line an engineering nightmare, with more than 20 bridges being required. Nonetheless, in the process some stunning views were afforded, few better than this on the sharp bend in the canal at **The Hyde**, where many postcard views were taken.
History of Wollaston Group

Left: Rather grandly, the tramway company called their terminus the **'Kinver Station.'** It was on Mill Lane, just down from The Vine Inn. Three concentric lines of track ended rather abruptly, parallel to the road. There, on August Bank Holiday Monday, 1925, the Kinver 'Symphony Orchestra' serenaded visitors! Today the terminus site is occupied by South Staffordshire Water's pumping station.
History of Wollaston Group

Left: **The Church of St Peter**, Kinver, is one of the finest parish churches for many a mile around. Its fabric is mainly early 14th century, incorporating some 12th century fragments from an earlier church. Substantial extensions were built in the mid-15th century, and by J.O. Scott restored the building in 1884-5 to designs by his father Sir George Gilbert Scott. In the 1970s, the need for repairs to the north aisle led to its imaginative reworking by local architect John Greaves Smith in 1976.

Right: On a Bank Holiday it was not uncommon for the Kinver Light Railway to bring in excess of 10,000 people to the village. They would make their way along Mill Lane into **High Street** to sample the delights of on offer, before heading to the Edge. This view of the Mill Lane end of High Street is contemporary to the tramway's operation, and was taken as a carnival procession made its way through the village.

Left: A look back along **Kinver High Street** in the early part of the 20th century. The White Harte, with a very prominent inn sign, can be seen at right, but otherwise the street is very quiet, apart from a single pony and trap and a few ambling pedestrians – no need for speed tables here!

Left: Life is little busier 40 or so years later, in this view almost 180° round from the one above. In the distance, half a dozen or so tourists are heading towards Kinver Edge.

Right: **Kinver High Street** has a timeless quality that can mislead one into thinking that it has changed little over the years. The reality is that there have been a number of buildings lost there over the years. These include Nos 101 - 104, seen here in 1965.

Left: **The Royal Exchange** is situated close to Stone Lane, where many tourists on foot would turn to head up to the Edge – an ideal spot for a pub where a bracer or two could be taken before tackling the climb. In the early 20th century the landlord was Frank Griffiths, and, here, one of the first cars in the area has paused for the camera. The elderly gentleman in the back has a very impressive beard!

Left: The soft sandstone on **Kinver Edge** is very easy to carve and cut into. This probably led to natural caves there being enlarged to form houses. People are recorded living in such dwellings as early as 1680. By far the greatest concentration of rock houses was around Holy Austin Rock, seen here. The name was derived from a former hermitage, known in the 15th century as 'Ostyn.'

Right: At its greatest extent, 10 or so families were living in the **rock houses**. In the early 20th century one of them was turned into a 'museum', where local curios were on display – for a small entrance charge. Here, a bearded troglodyte stares back at the camera from the doorway of the 'museum' house.

Left: The families living in the **rock houses** were re-housed in the early 1950s, but the 'museum' remained in use as a café until 1967. Thereafter the houses were abandoned, and fell prey to local vandals, some of whom attacked them with chainsaws. Luckily, the National Trust, who had responsibility for the Edge as a whole, took on the houses at Holy Austin Rock and restored them. Today they house displays and recreations of the original homes.

Left: Looking across Kinver towards Potter's Cross, with The Edge beyond, and the **Staffordshire & Worcestershire Canal** snaking though the image to the foreground. The Vine Inn is in the centre of the picture, whilst, to the far left, one of the three Kinver Light Railway toastrack cars (Nos 49-51) races to the terminus. This is possibly the only image to show one of these trams in motion.

Right: The Kinver trams could get crowded – but this is ridiculous! In fact it is not even Kinver. Generic postcards of this kind were produced nationally, and, with an overprint next to the word 'from', could appear to be from anywhere specified. This said, there were few places in the UK where trams were regularly so overloaded, especially at weekends and on Bank Holidays.

Left: The lull before the storm? A view inside Kinver 'Station' showing the concentric lines of track referred to on p139. On the extreme left is the exit to Mill Lane and the delights of Kinver. The destination blind on the tram behind the pointsman has been altered to read "FISH INN", the starting point for the tramway. So ends our journey through South Staffordshire. We hope you have enjoyed the trip – maybe we'll pass this way again?

Wolverhampton Archives & Local Studies

For the history of Bilston, Tettenhall, Penn, Wednesfield and Wolverhampton contact Wolverhampton Archives and Local Studies. We have books, manuscripts, photographs and other material going back over 500 years:

Parish registers, census returns, indexes to births, marriages and deaths, electoral registers, cemetery registers, school, business, charity and other archives as well as over 25,000 photographs.

Free access to the internet.

CD-ROM library and historical information sources e.g. WWI Deaths (660,000+ names), Oxford and Cambridge alumni 1261 – 1900 and many more!

Open - Mon, Tues, Fri 10.00 am – 5.00 pm, Wed 10.00am – 7.00 pm, closed on Thursdays, open 1st and 3rd Saturday each month 10.00 am – 5.00 pm

Visit our website for 100,000+ surname index entries, census street indexes, family tree tutorial and over 1000 pages of information relating to genealogy and local history.

www.wolverhampton.gov.uk/archives

42 – 50 Snow Hill
(opposite the Central Library)
Wolverhampton
WV2 4AG

Tel. 01902 552480

Email: **wolverhamptonarchives@dial.pipex.com**